UNDERW

A·D·V·E·N·T

50 of the Greatest!

Other books by Paul McCallum:

The Scuba Diving Handbook
A Practical Self-Defense Guide for Women
The Downhill Skiing Handbook (with Christine Lariviere McCallum)

UNDERWATER

A·D·V·E·N·T·U·R·E·S

50 of the Greatest!

Paul McCallum

BETTERWAY BOOKS
Cincinnati, Ohio

Cover design by Rick Britton
Cover photograph by Paul McCallum
Photographs by Paul McCallum

96 95 94 93 92   5 4 3 2 1

Library of Congress Cataloging-in-Publication Data

McCallum, Paul.
    Underwater adventures : 50 of the world's greatest/Paul McCallum
        p. cm.
    Includes index.
    ISBN 1-55870-255-5 : $16.95
    1. Diving, Submarine--Guidebooks. I. Title.
GV840.S78M3928 1992
    797.2--dc20   92-16482
                                                          CIP

This book is dedicated to
Christine Lariviere McCallum.

Acknowledgments

Scubahaus — for their continued support over the years.

Jon Hardy — companion on countless underwater adventures.

Lorraine Sadler — friend, underwater model, and companion on many dives.

Susan Morris — my talented and patient editor at Betterway.

Samantha Atkins — for her help in the preparation in this manuscript.

Robert F. Hostage and the staff at Betterway Publications.

Barry Krause — for his editing of the original manuscript.

Contents

Introduction

"Where should I go diving?"

"What can I do now that I'm certified?"

"What are some of the activities available if I get into diving?"

These are questions often asked by newly certified divers and people thinking about getting into diving. As an underwater photographer, I've been fortunate enough to have had the opportunity to travel to a variety of locations to sample, write about, and photograph the underwater environment. This book tries to answer the above questions based on some of the experiences I've had over the past few years.

There are also a few stories in the following text based on some of my friends' underwater adventures. Jon Hardy, for example, has served in almost every capacity possible within the dive industry — from executive director of NAUI to underwater insurance investigator. Ralph White of the Titanic Expeditions has had more deep water encounters of the high adventure type than anyone I know. Stories about their adventures are included for divers and non-divers alike.

Finally, it's my hope that by reading the following descriptions, you will gain a better understanding of what's available to the traveling diver. Underwater adventures can be had all over the world. Hopefully, this book can help you pick underwater adventures and locations that are right for you!

1 | Osborn Bank

"No one's ever been there ... at least as far I can tell," yelled Jon Hardy. He was yelling because the six- to eight- foot waves crashing over the bow of his twenty-eight-foot diveboat were drowning out his voice; we were also getting soaked. "If conditions get any worse we'll have to abort the dive," continued Jon. "It will be too hard to retrieve you from the water in all this chop."

Looking down at the "miles to destination" display on the boat's dash, I saw that it read a little over two miles; it seemed a shame to throw in the towel after coming so far. One of the things I've always admired about Jon Hardy is his ability to get me to places other skippers had told me were impossible to dive. On the other hand, if this man said it wasn't safe ... it wasn't.

We were on our way to Osborn Bank, which is located approximately thirteen miles off the backside of Catalina Island and about five miles off Santa Barbara Island. It is one of the many deep water pinnacles off the southern California Channel Islands.

Osborn was first brought to my attention after asking Jon if he could find the legendary "Matterhorn" pinnacle. According to information based on Jack McKenny's visit years ago, Matterhorn supposedly comes up from a few thousand feet and "peaks" at one hundred and thirty. The "peak" is said to be about ten feet wide — making Matterhorn a real underwater mountain!

Jon told me about Osborn along with a few other deep water pinnacles that could possibly fit the Matterhorn's profile. However, after a few questions with local fishermen, we learned that Osborn was a large flat area, which ruled it out as the Matterhorn. What was apparent about Osborn, however, was that no one knew anything about it.

Jon suddenly slowed the boat down, signaling our arrival at Osborn. The slowing of the boat was also the signal for Chipper Pastron and myself to move to the back of the boat while Lorraine Sadler and Jon went into their well-practiced routine.

"Three hundred ... 260 ... 180 ... 260 again." As Lorraine read off depth readings, Jon drove the boat around, attempting to find the high spot on the pinnacle, which the charts indicated was about 130.

Lorraine continued reading, "190 ... 200 ... 190 ... 170 ... and 160 ... 155."

"NOW!" yelled Jon.

Instantly, Lorraine had the anchor over the side and guided the rope through her hands as it plummeted towards the bottom. As the line ran out, Jon slowly backed up the boat to insure that the anchor "bit" into the bottom.

"We're here," smiled Jon, "and if you're going in, go now. If this swell picks up anymore, I won't be able to stay anchored without risking damage to the boat."

Lorraine, Chipper, and I began suiting up in the intense silence that proceeds an activity with a high adventure factor. People tend to get really focused at times like this since their senses are on full input. For me, it's one of the most enjoyable parts of the experience.

"See ya," said Chipper ... and then he backrolled into the water. The plan was to let Chipper have a ten-minute head start since he had been experiencing ear trouble lately. Rather than burn his air up (and ours waiting), Chipper took an extra tank with him to use to get down to thirty feet while his ears cleared. At thirty feet he would tie the tank off, switch to his own ninety-five cubic tank, and descend with Lorraine.

"See you on the bottom!" I said just before rolling into the water. Once in the water, the first order of business was to get up to the anchor line and drop below the surface as quickly as possible. Without a doubt, this was the roughest ocean I had ever been in, and I didn't want to get seasick just yet.

"Meet you on the bottom," yelled Lorraine, just before I started my descent. Lorraine has been my underwater model and dive companion for a number of years. What had started out as a purely recreational pursuit had become professional, and we now had quite a few magazine covers to our credit. Both of us were looking forward to shooting what we believed would be the first pictures of Osborn Bank.

At thirty feet I caught up to Chipper, who pointed to his ears and gave me an O.K. sign. After indicating that Lorraine was about a minute behind me, I started to descend once again along the anchor line.

My first thought was one of disappointment, since visibility was an extremely plankton-filled twenty to thirty feet. At 110 feet I stopped to take stock of how "narced" I was. Mildly, came the answer to myself, but still focused.

The temperature reading on my edge read 54 degrees, my S.P.G. read 2,400, and I knew where I was. All was well except for the lousy visibility. I still couldn't see bottom.

I continued down the anchor line until suddenly, at about 140 feet, it happened. Bang! Like a shot the bottom appeared below, and amazingly, the horizontal visibility opened up to over 160 feet!

The next surprise that hit me was the fact that *purple coral was everywhere*!

"Stay focused!" the voice in my head commanded. A quick look at my edge and S.P.G. told me I had over 2,000 psi, and about five minutes of no-decompression time left. After evaluating my current state of narcosis, I

Lorraine Sadler examines a large sea anemone in 160 feet of water at Osborn Bank.

cautiously, while watching the depth reading on my edge, followed the anchor line to the bottom, which met me at 155 feet.

"Stay focused! Check your S.P.G., check your edge!" once again came the mental commands. After complying, I looked up just in time to see a very enthusiastic-looking Chipper coming down the anchor line right behind a very focused-looking Lorraine.

"Don't get lost! Keep the anchor line in clear sight! Check your edge! Check your S.P.G.! Find something to take a picture of … quickly!"

Although I wanted to photograph the purple coral I had seen while descending, a quick look around revealed only a large red anemone within my immediate vicinity. Another glance at my edge revealed one minute of no-decompression time remaining, with 1,500 psi left in my tank. Time to take a picture!

Lorraine swam over to me with that "focused" look divers get when they are narced and know it. I pointed to her … and then to my own eyes with two fingers … and then to the red anemone. Meaning, "you look here." Lorraine, whom I've been communicating with underwater for sometime, immediately understood what I meant and posed, looking at the anemone.

"Check your edge!" came the voice. A quick look revealed an "up arrow" where the "time remaining" had been; this meant I had exceeded the no-decompression time and was adding to my decompression time with every second I stayed on the bottom.

"Take a picture now!" came the voice. Acting more on instinct than thought, I fired off two shots while Lorraine dutifully held her position.

"Check your S.P.G.!" yelled the voice. A quick glance at my air gauge revealed that I had a little over 1,000 psi left. "Take one more shot and get out of here," said the voice. So, after firing off one more shot of Lorraine and the anemone, I pointed to myself and then gave her the thumbs up signal, meaning "I'm going up, see ya."

With one hand on my edge, and the other on the anchor line, I began my ascent towards the surface. At around one hundred feet, the effects of nitrogen narcosis were pretty much gone. At eighty feet, the up arrow on my edge disappeared and the "Time Remaining" display returned. That always brought a sense of relief since it meant a direct ascent to the surface was now possible if an emergency were to occur.

"Check your S.P.G.," instructed the voice. At fifty feet, with about 700 psi left, and the hang-off tank now visible up ahead, bouncing twenty-five feet below the boat, the dive was basically over. All that remained was a long safety stop, which would be spent watching the pixels pull back on my edge.

2 | The President Coolidge

"It's the biggest shipwreck in the world!" said Robin, who was calling from *Fisheye View Magazine* in Florida. "At least it's the biggest one in shallow enough water to be visited on scuba."

Robin was generously offering me a chance to write a story about the wreck of the *President Coolidge* for her magazine. Naturally, I accepted!

A little research revealed that the *President Coolidge*, at 654 feet, truly is the biggest shipwreck in the world within the reach of conventional sport diving equipment. There are bigger wrecks, such as the *Titanic*, but you're not going to get there with a scuba tank.

Traveling to the *President Coolidge* is an adventure in itself! The usual itinerary involves first getting yourself to New Zealand. From New Zealand, you will fly via Air Vanuatu to Port Vila on Efate Island, Vanuatu. From Port Vila, you'll board a boat for the two-day journey to the island of Espiritu Santo, which is where the *Coolidge* is located.

I highly recommend the live-aboard diveboat *Coriolis* in Vanuatu. The 140-foot *Coriolis* will pick you up in Port Vila and provide you with the opportunity to visit and dive other islands during your stay in Vanuatu.

The Accident

On the morning of October 26, 1942, the converted luxury liner *President Coolidge* was sailing off the island of Espiritu Santo. In her new capacity as a troop transport, she had over 5,000 U.S. troops on-board.

As the ship entered the channel leading to the harbor, the captain was handed a message that had just come over the radio from Allied troops onshore; it read, "DANGER … YOU ARE ENTERING A MINE FIELD!"

Before he had finished reading the message, the ship was rocked by an explosion. The captain ordered full astern, but the ship didn't change direction fast enough to avoid hitting a second mine. Within minutes, the *Coolidge* began listing to port. Realizing his ship was going to sink, the captain ran her aground and gave the order to abandon ship. Huge nets were lowered over the side to provide an escape route for the soldiers and crew.

Evacuation of the ship was slow because most of the crew didn't believe the ship was in danger of sinking, since she had been run aground. Also, the water had become covered with oil; solders on the bottom of the nets were hanging on because they didn't want to jump into the oil.

An hour after hitting the mines, the *Coolidge* was listing dangerously. The shift in the ship's attitude caused her to slip off the sand bar and slide

Wrecks become artificial reefs and provide shelter for a variety of marine life.

into deeper water where the danger of sinking became a sudden reality. Orders were given to kick into the water anyone hanging onto the bottom of the evacuation nets. A group of soldiers had become trapped in the ship's galley. Unable to escape due to the ship's listing and onrushing sea water, they would have perished if it had not been for the heroic efforts of Army Captain Elwood J. Euart.

Captain Euart tied a rope around his waist and lowered himself to the trapped men through a sea wall in the ship's hull. After helping each man to the rope, where they climbed out, Captain Euart attempted to climb out himself. Sadly, he had become too weak to save himself and went down with the ship before he could be helped.

Miraculously, there were only two fatalities when the *Coolidge* went down. Besides Captain Euart, Fireman Robert Ried died from the explosion when the ship hit the first mine. Two hours after hitting the mines, at approximately 10:30 A.M., the *Coolidge* slipped beneath the waves.

Ship's History

The *President Coolidge* was built by the Donner Steam Ship Line in the late 1920s. She was 654 feet long, weighed 22,000 tons, and cost 8 million dollars to construct. Launched in 1931, the ship was named after the thirtieth president of the United States and was christened by his wife, Mrs. Calvin Coolidge.

Air transport had yet to become a feasible means of transpacific travel in the early 1930s. The Donner Line built the *President Coolidge* to supply a fast means of travel between the United States and the Orient. On her maiden voyage, the *Coolidge* carried 12,000 passengers across the Pacific in what was then a record-setting time of twelve days. For almost ten years she routinely made the crossing from her home port in San Francisco.

The bombing of Pearl Harbor in 1941 brought the United States into World War II. Thousands of troops and support equipment needed transportation to the South Pacific. Like many other ships of her time, the *Coolidge* was stripped of most of her luxuries and converted into a troop transport.

Diving the Coolidge

At 654 feet, the *President Coolidge* is 150 feet longer than the biggest ship in Truk Lagoon (the *Shinkoku Maru*). Due to its size, you should plan on spending a few days diving the *Coolidge*.

The *Coolidge* can be dove from either shore or boat; there are two lines that will lead you to the bow in seventy feet of water. One runs from a buoy on the surface; the other runs from a decompression/safety stop area in fifteen feet of water just offshore. Because of the depths involved on the

A lone crinoid sits on a Gorgonian on a wall off Vanuatu in the South Pacific.

Coolidge, it is a good idea always to ascend along the line that leads to the safety stop area at fifteen feet. A hang-on bar has been anchored with cement where the line ends. I found this arrangement to be very convenient.

There are two forward cargo holds; both are filled with tires, jeeps, large cables, and piles of other automotive debris. Depth in the forward hold is about one hundred feet.

The *Coolidge* lies on her port (left) side. When swimming along the wreck, you may find it helpful to acclimate yourself to the ship's new position. I found a large artillery gun outside the second cargo hold that I almost missed because my perspective was off.

On the right side of the hull near the bow, there is a fairly large gun mounted to the deck. Just below the gun, I consistently found a large group of scorpionfish. Certain areas of the wreck are home to high populations of these unusual fish.

Beyond the second cargo hold lies the towering superstructure. If you enter on the shallower right side of the hull, you can swim down a long hallway and still have large areas of open water overhead. Rifles, helmets, and other military debris can be found in this corridor.

After swimming two-thirds the way down the hull, your guide (do dive with a guide or you will never find this stuff) will lead you deeper inside the wreck to a large room with a fireplace. Above the fireplace sits "the lady," a statue of a woman standing in front of a horse. Depth at the lady is 160. Do not attempt this dive without a guide.

Above and behind the lady, in 140 feet of water, lie the rows of toilets that were put in when the *Coolidge* was converted to a troop carrier. Swimming beyond the toilets takes you past a tiled fountain and back out the front of the superstructure just below where you entered. It would take weeks of diving to see all the *Coolidge* has to offer. In addition to the lady, the swimming pool and soda fountain are also worth seeing.

3 | The R.M.S. Rhone

The R.M.S. ("Royal Mail Steamer") *Rhone*, located off Salt Island in the British Virgin Islands, is another shipwreck well worth visiting. She is also one of the most well-known shipwrecks in the world and has been used as an underwater location for numerous films, including *The Deep*, starring Jacqueline Bisset.

The 310-foot *Rhone* was built in 1865 by the Millwall Iron Works in England. She was primarily a steamship, but, like many ships of her time, could also be powered by sail.

On October 29, 1867, the *Rhone* was anchored off Peter Island in the British Virgin Islands when a fierce hurricane hit without much warning. Captain Wooley attempted to pull anchor and sail to the safety of open water. Unfortunately, the anchor and chain became entangled, delaying the ship's escape. When the 300 feet of chain and anchor finally tore free of the ship, it was too late. As Captain Wooley tried to make sail for the safety of open water, the storm swept the *Rhone* onto the rocks off Salt Island and split her in half.

Today the *Rhone* rests on a sloping sandy bottom with the bow in seventy-four feet of water and the stern in about twenty-five. The area has been declared a National Park so that nothing may be removed from the wreck.

As with most wrecks, the *Rhone* requires a couple dives to really see all she has to offer. Most divers visit the deeper bow area first, which is one of the most photogenic sites on the wreck. A small signaling cannon sits pinned under the ship's frame in this area.

If you leave the bow and swim towards the midsection of the ship, you will reach the first mast. Macro-photographers will appreciate the numerous tubeworms that can be found growing here. If you make a night dive on the wreck, check crevices on the mast for sleeping parrotfish.

The midsection of the *Rhone* is in about sixty feet of water and will probably be recognizable to you from pictures you have seen in the past. This area is referred to as "the pillars" because of the Roman-looking pillars created by the ship's framework. Photo opportunities are literally everywhere in this area.

The stern of the *Rhone* sits in about twenty-five feet of water. Photographic opportunities are abundant, with the ship's large propeller and rudder being the main attractions.

Tom Maney examines the bow section of the R.M.S. Rhone.

4 | The Chikuzen

The *Chikuzen* is also located in the British Virgin Islands and is a terrific follow-up wreck after visiting the *Rhone*. In addition to being an outstanding dive on her own merit, it is also interesting to see the differences between a ship that has been underwater for twelve years (the *Chikuzen*) and one that's been submerged for almost 120 (the *Rhone*).

The *Chikuzen's* fate was sealed on August 11, 1981, when a hurricane was reported to be approaching the British Virgin Islands. To avoid damage to the harbor by the *Chikuzen's* bulky hull, her owners towed the 223-foot-long ship into open water, where they attempted to sink her by setting the ship on fire ... only she didn't sink. Instead, she became a safety hazard and drifted back towards the harbor.

An industrious local diver came to the rescue and towed the burning ship to her final resting place eight miles north of Scrub Island. Amazingly, the task of towing the 223-foot burning ship was accomplished with a twenty-foot diveboat ... at a speed of one-half knot an hour!

The fact that the *Chikuzen* is located in open water contributes to her being one of the best wreck dives in the Caribbean. The wreck has become a living reef in an otherwise barren environment and offers protection to a wide variety of marine species.

Large stingrays with wing spans of seven feet or more can be found resting on the sandy bottom around the wreck. Schools of barracuda made up of hundreds of individuals are common. Blacktip reef sharks are occasionally seen; I've never seen such dense populations of yellow grunts as can be found on the *Chikuzen*.

A school of grunts swims along the wreck of Chikuzen *in the British Virgin Islands.*

5 | The Cuan Law

Before you can dive the R.M.S. *Rhone* or the *Chikuzen*, you will first need to travel to the sites by boat. Most divers feel that the Trimarine Boat Company's *Cuan Law* is unquestionably the best choice of transport.

The *Cuan Law* is the biggest trimaran in the world ... she also is possibly the most comfortable diveboat in the world. With a length of 105 feet, a beam of 44, and a height of 103 feet, the *Cuan Law* is an impressive sight. Her owners/designers, Duncan and Annie Muirhead, spent considerable time researching what type of vessel would be the most comfortable for divers and vacationers. They chose a trimaran because the ship's generators, engines, crew quarters, galley, and storage could all be placed (and are) in the ship's pontoons. This arrangement allows the main deck to be used solely for guest cabins and lounges.

Comfort on the *Cuan Law*, however, goes way beyond cabin size. The way the ship is run contributes to the *Cuan Law* experience. For example, *at night the ship is anchored and all generators are turned off.* Anyone who has spent a night trying to sleep in a tiny bunk ... while their boat is moved during the night in rough seas can appreciate this! Add to this scenario the incessant noise created by a ship's engines and generators, and it's easy to see why many people can't sleep on a boat! On the *Cuan Law*, nights are silent and peaceful.

All meals on the *Cuan Law* are prepared by the ship's cook, Jan McCoy, and they are terrific! The dinner menu when I was on-board consisted of entrées such as roast beef, swordfish, and stuffed chicken, each served with vegetables, potatoes, salads, and a different wine. Lunches included tacos, pizza, and a huge array of cold cuts and homemade breads. Jan's chocolate desserts alone are worth the trip!

There are ten double occupancy cabins on the *Cuan Law*. One feature that adds considerably to passenger comfort is the fact that *each cabin has its own toilet, shower, and wash basin.* This was a first for me. On every other diveboat I've ever been on, showers and toilets were shared by a number of cabins.

Lack of an adequate supply of fresh water is a problem on many ships. The *Cuan Law* solves this by carrying two 600-gallon tanks in addition to a water maker. This arrangement assures round-the-clock fresh water for all guests.

Food on Cuan Law *is absolutely first-class.*

Non-Diving Activities

The *Cuan Law* offers many activities other than diving. This fact makes a week on *Cuan Law* an ideal "family vacation." The trip I was on there was a young couple on their honeymoon. He liked to dive ... and she didn't. On a boat other than *Cuan Law*, she would have spent her week watching bubbles. However, *Cuan Law* has twenty-two mountain bikes at its disposal. The couple spent two of their afternoons mountain biking on nearby islands while some of us went diving. Other days found them windsurfing, water-skiing, hiking/rock climbing, and picnicking. One man's teenage son practically gave up diving once he discovered the ship's knee board.

The point is there are *lots of non-diving activities* associated with a vacation on *Cuan Law*. Personally, I found just sailing around very relaxing. A typical itinerary includes two dives in the morning with a non-diving activity in the afternoon.

Water-skiing is only one of the many activities offered vacationers on Cuan Law.

6 | Diving for Abalone

Few things are as delicious as a plate of freshly caught and prepared abalone! In fact, in many parts of the world abalone diving has become a local tradition.

Catching an abalone is easy since they don't swim ... and move at a snail's pace. You will, however, need to purchase an *ab iron* to pry the animals off the rocks. Abalone are hemophiliac and thus incapable of healing once they are cut ... so they will bleed to death. An ab iron allows you to remove the animal from the rock it lives on without damaging it so that if it measures "undersize" you can "replant" it without damage. Do not use a dive knife since this will cause irreparable damage that will eventually kill the animal.

There are strict laws governing how many abalone you may take, where you may take them, when you may take them, and how big they must be. To avoid heavy fines, be sure to check local fish and game regulations.

Species of Abalone

Depending on whom you talk with, there are either seven or eight species of abalone. Some scientists feel that the threaded abalone is actually a subspecies of the *pinto*.

Identifying the various species underwater can be difficult at first because all abalone basically look alike. The numbers of holes, or "pores," in the shell can provide clues, as can the color of the animal's tentacles, and the color and contour of the shell. The eight species of abalone found in California are:

Black Abalone: The black abalone is one of the most common species and is often the first one to be encountered by novice hunters; it's also one of the smaller species, growing to about five inches.

Black abs are so named because of their black to dark blue shells. For some reason, the shells of black abalone are usually not covered with encrusting organisms, and the inside of the shell is pearly white. There are between five and nine open pores in the shell. The animal's tentacles are black.

Green Abalone: The green abalone is also common in many areas of southern California's Channel Islands. The animal's shell is green or brownish-green with five to seven open pores, which are elevated a little off the shell. The tentacles of green abalone are also green. Green abs grow to a maximum size of about ten inches. Generally, green abs are found in shallow water.

Lorraine Sadler displays a local California abalone.

Pink Abalone: The pink abalone also grows to about ten inches. The shell is dark green or reddish-green with two to four open pores elevated above the shell. The animal's tentacles are black, and the inside of the shell is pinkish.

The shell of the pink abalone has a wavy pattern running across it, which may help in identification. Unfortunately, if the shell is covered with encrusting organisms, the pattern may be obscured.

Red Abalone: The red abalone, which grows to almost twelve inches, is the world's largest. The exterior of the shell is reddish with three to four open pores. The animal's tentacles are black, and the inside of the shell is greenish.

White Abalone: The white abalone is generally found in deep water (eighty feet and deeper) and grows to a maximum size of ten inches. The white abalone is the grand prize of ab hunters and is said to be exceptionally delicious.

The reddish-white shell is covered with small bumps that, depending on the amount of encrusting organisms on the shell, may aid in field identification. There are three to five open pores elevated above the shell. The animal's tentacles are light green, and the inside of the shell is pearly white with traces of pink.

Pinto Abalone: Pinto abalone grow to about six inches and aren't found in southern California; at least I've yet to see one there. They are, however, commercially fished in Canada and Alaska.

The shell is dark brown with three to six open pores. The animal's tentacles are greenish-brown and the inside of the shell is pearly white.

Flat Abalone: The flat abalone grow to about six inches. Its shell is dark red, sometimes reddish white; there are five to six open pores. The animal's tentacles are yellowish-green, and the inside of the shell is purplish pink. The shells of flat abalone have a bumpy surface similar to white abalone.

Threaded Abalone: The shell of the threaded abalone has a wavy texture, similar to the pink abalone. There are four to six open pores and the animal's tentacles are yellowish-green. The inside of the shell is pearly white.

7 | A Cold Water Surprise

El Niño, a weather condition that results in warm water coming up from the tropics, often causes unusual marine life to show up off Catalina.

One of the most unusual encounters took place during a recent El Niño. At the time, Jon, Mike, and Lorraine were busy working the harbor — repairing various broken pieces of marine equipment that had been damaged during the storm.

"What's wrong with that mooring?" Lorraine asked, pointing to one of the mooring's pick-up poles that was half-submerged and bobbing like a float on a fishing pole. "It looks as if something's caught in it."

Jon skillfully maneuvered the twenty-five-foot *Argo* into position next to the mooring while Lorraine prepared to get in the water.

"What is that!?" yelled Mike, suddenly sounding nervous. "There's something huge down there ... it must be ten feet wide and over ten feet long ... it looks like a giant black square!" Scuba diving was clearly not on Mike's top ten list of things to do at this particular moment. Lorraine, on the other hand, didn't hesitate to jump right in.

"What is she ... nuts? That thing looks like it's about to come up! What if it's hungry?"

A few moments later, Lorraine surfaced. "It's a manta ray and it's tangled up in the mooring line ... I'm going to cut it loose." Considering the fact that this was the middle of winter and the water temperature usually averaged a chilly 58 to 62 degrees, a manta ray was indeed a rare sight. The animal had wandered up from the tropics, probably a result of the unusual conditions brought about by El Niño.

Grabbing his video camera in one hand and Nikonos in the other, Jon joined Lorraine in the water and began filming as she gently began untangling the ray. After about twenty minutes, she finally managed to release the creature.

A new problem immediately became apparent. Although able to swim weakly, the manta ray kept swimming to the surface, where it would "hover" for some time. The concern was that the boat traffic within the harbor might accidentally run over the animal and damage it.

The decision was made to go to shore to pick up a local biologist who had heard about what was going on and wanted to come out to observe the ray.

"Grab me some film," yelled Jon to Lorraine as she ran off to get fresh tanks. "There's piles of it in the fridge," continued Jon, referring to the hundred plus roles of film he kept in his refrigerator.

A few minutes later, the group was reassembled on the *Argo* and heading back out to the ray. "Let me have the film," requested Jon, as he took the exposed film out of his Nikonos.

"Here you go," said Lorraine as she handed Jon *one* roll of film.

"Where's the rest?" Jon asked, surprised he was being handed only one roll of film.

"That's all I brought," a bewildered Lorraine responded. It seems that in the excitement of the moment she had done exactly as asked. Jon asked for some film … so Lorraine brought him "a roll" of film!

A few minutes later the group returned to the site where they had left the manta ray. The animal was still swimming weakly near the surface and didn't seem to understand how to get back to open water. To assist the ray, Lorraine and Mike entered the water, and each grabbed one side of the animal and guided it out of the harbor by "swimming" it along. Jon shot some amazing video footage of the whole event, which has since been used in various films.

Once the ray was clear of the harbor, it seemed to come to life. Within moments, the animal assertively swam into the safety of open water.

8 | Angel Sharks

"You can actually pick them up!" said Jon, as the two of us were gearing up for a dive at Ship Rock.

"Pick up a sleeping shark?" This sounded like a bad idea, but since Jon Hardy had never led me on anything but safe and exciting underwater adventures, I completely trusted him.

As we began our descent, it was easy to see why local divers claim Ship Rock to be one of the best dives in southern California. Located about a mile off the Isthmus on the front side of Catalina, Ship Rock offers a diverse selection of marine life and environment. From the surface to 130 feet (where the rock ends and a steeply sloping, sandy bottom begins), the bottom terrain is made up of large boulders and a lush kelp bed. Large pelagic animals, such as schooling sharks and other deep-water species, are occasionally seen as they pass the island. Spearfishermen enjoy the abundant game fish: barracuda, sheepshead, yellowtail, and kelp bass. Photographers will find an abundance of subjects ranging from the above mentioned fish to numerous macro-subjects such as nudibranchs, anemones, shellfish, and tubeworms.

One of the highlights of Ship Rock is the wreckage of a sailboat that recently ran aground while participating in a regatta from the mainland to Catalina. Most of the wreckage can be found scattered around the bottom in thirty feet of water. The hull has broken in two and lies in various locations around the sloping bottom from twenty to sixty feet. The mast and other parts of the superstructure offer photographic opportunities.

The real highlight of Ship Rock, however, is the angel sharks that can be found at the base of the rock in deeper water. As Jon and I hovered at 150 feet, we could make out the outlines of at least a dozen angel sharks on the bottom. Gently, Jon slipped his hands under the two wing-like lobes on either side of the animal's body. To my amazement, the four-and-one-half foot shark didn't wake up as Jon slowly lifted the animal clear of the sand and held it while I shot a roll of film. I wouldn't recommend trying this unless you are under the supervision of a qualified guide.

"Have you ever been bitten?" I asked Jon after our dive.

"Yes," he replied. "The thing is, angel sharks aren't usually aggressive, but they do have teeth and *can* draw blood. They tend to chew something once they bite into it. One of the times I was bitten happened when I approached an animal head-on to observe it from the front. Without warning, the shark suddenly bolted up, smacked me in the face, and knocked my mask off in addition to tearing my regulator out of my mouth.

It then proceeded to get tangled up in my regulator hose, which it decided to chew on. The problem was that the animal absolutely refused to let me have it back. Fortunately, I had an alternate second stage and so put that in my mouth while slowly ascending to the surface with this four-foot angel shark chewing on my regulator hose. Once near the surface, the animal suddenly let go and swam away."

Jon Hardy can lift these sleeping angel sharks without waking them — supplying divers with unique photo opportunities.

9 | Conception Island

Conception Island is one of the least-known islands in the Bahamas ... it's also one of the best as far as divers are concerned. Located south of Cat Island and east of San Salvador, Conception Island is so small that it is not on many maps. The only way to visit the island is by boat. The *Coral Star* is one boat that runs regularly scheduled trips to the island.

Two outstanding dives are *The Cathedral* and *The Mangrove*. The Cathedral is a wall dive that starts in about sixty feet of water. Sections of the wall are circular and resemble an amphitheater decorated with gigantic clusters of purple tube sponges. The majestic sponges are what inspired the dive site's name. Another aspect of the Cathedral that makes it an exciting dive is the numerous stingrays that inhabit the sandy bottom. As soon as you enter the water, you will be able to see at least a dozen stingrays of various sizes, swimming lazily beneath the boat. These animals are slowly becoming accustomed to divers from the *Coral Star* and will allow divers to feed and pet them. Obviously, this should only be done under the supervision of a qualified guide.

Visibility at the Cathedral is at least 150 feet, with 200-foot visibility not uncommon. Water temperature is 75 degrees during the winter and an average 80 degrees during the summer.

Since the Cathedral is a deep-water dive (in most places along the wall, I was unable to see the bottom), there is an excellent chance you will encounter sharks, large barracuda, and other big animals. This is one reason photographers should make a point of visiting this site.

The Mangrove is another site off Conception Island where the chances of encountering big animals are high. The water in the Mangrove is shallow and warm ... an ideal environment for young and small fish. Predators have learned that the mouth of the Mangrove is an excellent feeding ground when the tide runs out. I was amazed to find numerous spotted eagle rays and several large barracuda "cruising" the mouth of the Mangrove. Photographic opportunities abound because the animals seem to view skin-divers as simply other predators looking to feed on the smaller animals. In fact, this is often the case in any "feeding" situation.

The Bahamas are made up of a 1,000-mile chain of 700 islands that cover 100,000 square miles of water. Bimini, located fifty-two miles off the coast of Florida, is the closest of these islands to the U.S. Like Conception Island, there are a lot of unknown (as far as divers are concerned) islands in the Bahamas chain. If you have access to a boat, you may want to spend a few days exploring new dive sites.

Clusters of purple tube sponges ... typical of the underwater beauty off Conception Island.

The sun deck on Coral Star *is comfortable and spacious.*

Staterooms on Coral Star *are extremely comfortable.*

10 Rum Cay Island

The only way to visit Rum Cay is by boat. There was a dive resort on the island, but it was recently closed.

Located slightly east of Long Island and south of San Salvador, Rum Cay offers divers a diverse mixture of deep wall dives, shallow reef dives, and abundant snorkeling opportunities. One of the most spectacular dives off Rum Cay is *Sandy Point*, on the northwest side of the island. The wall starts in fifty feet of water and drops down well below safe sport diving depths. Large elephant ear sponges are the highlight for sightseers and photographers alike. Some of the sponges are twenty feet in diameter and are capable of dwarfing a diver!

Another excellent dive well worth visiting is *Samantha's Reef*, located just south of the Christian Science Center. Fish photographers will love this place. Various species of butterflyfish, angelfish, flatfish, and red and rock hinds are common, as are the numerous parrotfish that can be found in various stages of maturity. Depth is in the thirty-foot range and is made up of coral heads and scattered sandy areas. Barracuda are extremely common, as are the basket sponges that are common to the area.

Coral Bay Cruises runs trips to Rum Cay on-board their boat, the *Coral Star*. The *Coral Star* is 115 feet long, 22 feet wide, and weighs 230 tons. The boat is capable of servicing eighteen passengers and offers a variety of accommodations. The three master cabins have a queen-size bed in a large room, along with a private bathroom. These cabins are definitely some of the most comfortable I have encountered on a live-aboard diveboat. The ship's two deluxe cabins offer a large single lower bed with a smaller bunk bed above. The deluxe cabins also have a private bathroom. The less expensive cabins are referred to as the "standard" staterooms and sleep two passengers per room; two rooms share one bathroom.

The *Coral Star* carries 5,800 gallons of fresh water and is capable of making an additional 1,200 gallons of fresh water a day. Anyone who has had to worry about water rationing while at sea can appreciate the large amount of water *Coral Star* carries!

Diving is done directly from *Coral Star*, and the captain is extremely conscientious about where he drops the ship's anchor. The boat does have a twenty-two-foot diesel launch and a twelve-foot inflatable to shuttle divers to and from shore.

With a range of 4,000 miles, the *Coral Star* is a good choice for divers who wish to visit the Bahamas, Turk and Caicos Islands, or other islands in the vicinity.

11 | Shark Diving

"Sharks do the worst thing possible. They eat you alive ... and they do it when you are alone!"

The above statement was made by *Jaws'* author Peter Benchley, who at the time was talking about man's primitive fear of sharks; he summed it up well. The fear of being eaten alive is very primal. Modern man doesn't live with the fear of a tiger coming into his cave to eat him, nor are most of us likely to get jumped by a hungry grizzly bear on our way to work. Sharks are really the last potentially dangerous animal that modern man can still accidentally encounter face to face ... and possibly get eaten alive in the process.

The other day I was explaining to a group of people how unlikely it was that a diver would get bitten while shark diving. I explained that the sharks are looking for the source of food scent we have put in the water and so don't pay much attention to the divers. My brother, Val, replied at this point, "Hey babe, *you* are the food source in the water!"

It would be wise to remember those words when shark diving. Don't ever get overconfident — always treat the animals with the respect that a big predator who can "eat you alive" deserves!

If you want to go shark diving, contact one of the resorts or boat operators who specialize in these types of trips. Do not under any circumstances go out and try this on your own!

The first step of any shark trip is to take a boat out into open water. Jon Hardy of Catalina's Argo Diving Service has run numerous shark trips and believes you need to be a minimum of five miles away from land to attract any serious shark action.

Another consideration is that local sun bathers, surfers, and swimmers won't invite you to their July Fourth barbecue if you are responsible for chumming up a small school of sharks a few hundred yards beyond the surf line!

After the boat is ten miles or so offshore, the next step is to place the shark cage in the water. Some shark trip operators first chum the water, and then put the cage in the water when the sharks show up. Depending on the type of cage used and the species of sharks you are dealing with, this order of operation may be acceptable.

For example, a blue shark trip may involve jumping in the water and swimming to a cage that may be sixty feet or so away from the boat. In that scenario, it's safer to set the cage up in advance. On a great white shark trip, however, divers prudently choose to jump through the top of the cage from the deck of the boat. With the cage so near the boat, setup time is shorter and therefore more important … it doesn't require that a diver get in the water to set it up.

Once the cage is in the water, it is time to "chum." Chumming means to place a scent in the water that will attract sharks. Every shark trip I've been on has used frozen whole mackerel as chum. The frozen fish are placed in a "goodie bag" and then stabbed with a knife a few times. With larger fish it is a good idea to hammer them with a knife a couple of times before putting them in the bag. The idea is make sure the fish are releasing "scent" when they are placed in the water. The bag of fish is placed inside two milk crates that are then strapped together. This protects the bag from being ripped apart when the sharks show up.

Since most shark trips take place in open water where the ocean's depth may be several thousand feet, the boat isn't anchored, but is allowed to drift. In some instances a "sea anchor" may be used to slow down the drift.

Now that the chum is in the water all you do is wait for the sharks. It's not uncommon to have to wait several hours before the first shark shows up. On all the shark trips I've been on it has taken at least two hours before any animals arrived. However, once the first shark comes in, others quickly follow. There may be forty or more sharks around your boat after a few hours!

I should say here that my experience with chumming is limited primarily to blue sharks and a few makos. Expeditions seeking great white sharks often chum for days or even weeks before meeting with success. On the other hand, many tropical species of sharks are routinely seen during "non-shark" dives. Divers in Palau, for example, encounter blacktip reef sharks on almost every dive.

When the sharks do show up, it's time for the moment of truth … the next step is to jump in the water with the hungry sharks! Chances are you may have to swim to the cage with an "armed" escort diver. Few underwater experiences are as exciting as your first swim through shark-infested waters!

Once you are in the cage, stay there. Resist any temptation you may feel to leave the cage and swim with the sharks. Remember that you are in deep open water; the cage, in addition to providing protection, also serves as a reference point. If you swim freely, you may lose track of where the boat is, what your depth is, and other information important to your safety.

Oddly enough, my funniest moment underwater took place during one of my first shark dives. Cinematographer Howard Hall had invited me to come along for two days while he shot some footage of blue sharks for one of his nature films.

Howard Hall films a blue shark off San Diego.

At one point during the second day of dives, I found myself alone in the water with a bunch of blue sharks. This wasn't a concern, however, since I felt secure from my safe vantage point inside the cage. The only place of entry to the cage is through the front where a section of bars can be lifted upward to allow divers to enter. This sliding "window" also allows photographers to shoot pictures without having the cage bars in the way. If a shark tries to swim into the cage, you simply push it away.

My one concern was that one of the smaller sharks might be thin enough to swim in between the bars. I had also been instructed not to look behind me, but to keep my attention focused forward where the sliding window was. This, I was told, was where a shark might possibly enter the cage if I didn't pay attention!

With the sliding window in the upper "open" position, I was happily taking pictures while feeling like quite the marine explorer when off in the distance appeared a large, long, "thick"-looking object swimming straight towards the cage with torpedo-like speed. Blue sharks swim in a snake-like "S" style, curving their entire body as they slowly wind their way towards you. The shark that was bearing down on my cage was a whole different ball game. Besides swimming in a straight line, using only its tail for propulsion, the speed it was traveling at was frightening. Suddenly, taking pictures was less of a priority than shutting the cage window — which came banging down just before I had my first closeup view of a mako shark. The animal sped by my cage, swam two large circles around it ... and left.

A few seconds after the shark disappeared, I felt, much to my horror, the vise-like jaws of a shark closing around my right buttock. My heart froze in terror as I tried to launch myself out of my wet suit, and out of the cage! As I spun around to fend off my attacker, I came face to face not with a blue shark ... but with Howard Hall, who was laughing so hard he couldn't stop his mask from flooding. It seems he had entered the water just in time to see me eagerly close the cage window as the mako approached. I hadn't been bitten by a shark, but had been grabbed by an underwater prankster!

12 | Pinnipeds

"Here comes another squad!" yelled Chipper, as a pod of sea lions raced towards him. Lorraine, Jon Hardy, and I always enjoyed diving with Chipper, since his enthusiasm for diving was contagious.

"A squad?" Lorraine queried, as she looked back at Jon and me. As usual, Chip was coming up with his own terminology for the marine environment.

Not wanting to miss the photo opportunity that was rapidly developing as the sea lions approached from one direction while a small school of white-sided dolphins closed in from open water, I grabbed my camera and jumped in.

Sea lions (*Zalophus californicus*) can be differentiated from seals in two ways. First, sea lions have external *ears* ... seals don't. The second way to tell them apart is by the size and use of their *foreflippers*. Seals can't turn their foreflippers forward ... sea lions can, which gives sea lions greater mobility on land. Also, sea lions use their foreflippers as their main means of propulsion through the water, while seals use their rear flippers as the main means of propulsion. The trained "seals" in circuses are usually sea lions.

Part of the family of pinnipeds that also includes Steller's sea lions, harbor seals, elephant seals, fur seals, and sea otters, sea lions feed primarily on fish and squid; they usually live along rocky shorelines. Males can reach lengths of ten feet and weigh in at 700 pounds, while females average eight feet and weigh in at 250 pounds. Usually, the females are the ones that approach within inches of divers.

Seals generally aren't as gregarious as sea lions, and so they are harder to get close to in the water. Occasionally, individuals will be encountered that seem to thrive on human contact. Once, during three days of diving, a mature female harbor seal followed me around and actually let me pet her. The animal would even wait around the boat for us to enter the water. A scientist friend of mine theorized that the animal may have been released from some type of training or rescue program and missed human contact.

Elephant seals are the largest of the pinnipeds, reaching lengths of sixteen feet and weighing a few thousand pounds. Named after the male's bulbous, elephant-like snout, elephant seals are not as common in southern California as sea lions are. Some of the state's northern Channel Islands, such as San Miguel, have large breeding populations of elephant seals.

Fur seals were once hunted for their coats, which brought their worldwide population down to 125,000 — the brink of extinction. Fortunately, they have been a protected species since 1911, and there are now well over one million individuals in the U.S. alone.

Sea otters are one of the most delightful marine animals a diver can encounter. Once hunted for their reddish brown coats, sea otters were also brought to the brink of extinction before becoming a protected species in 1913. Currently, the population is relatively strong and has been increasing by roughly five percent a year.

White sharks feed on pinnipeds. Perhaps, if you are lucky, you will encounter white sharks while diving with these animals!

Sea lions wait for divers to enter the water off San Nicholas Island.

Divers relax between dives at La Ceiba Hotel.

13 Cozumel

Cozumel is located off the eastern tip of Mexico's Yucatan Peninsula and offers some of the best wall diving in the world. The island is about thirty miles long and ten miles wide. The main (and only) town of San Miguel is set midway down the western side of Cozumel and is dedicated to the tourist trade. All hotels and dive sites are on the western side of the island. I've never experienced anything except great diving in Cozumel; some of the more memorable sites include:

Santa Rosa Wall: Big fish, a strong current, deep water, and colorful sponges sum up Santa Rosa Wall. Actually, they should call this place the Santa Rosa Cliff! The wall starts in about sixty feet ... and you can forget about trying to find the bottom.

The current at Santa Rosa runs south to north (as it does at most of Cozumel's sites) and is strong enough that staying in one place is impractical, if not impossible. I found the best way to dive Santa Rosa Wall is to drift with the current without swimming ... and then let the fish approach me. This is one dive on which you might consider bringing two cameras.

The visibility at Santa Rosa Wall averages 150 feet! Currents around Cozumel are strong and have a cleansing effect by continually bringing in fresh, clear water from the depths. The terrific visibility, combined with the fact that Cozumel has a *year-round water temperature of 81 degrees Fahrenheit*, contributes to the reasons why divers continually make return trips to Cozumel. For instance, I hate wearing a wet suit ... and you can leave your wet suit at home when visiting Cozumel. Also, the air temperature is a pretty constant 90 degrees Fahrenheit, so you can leave your jackets, sweaters, and other heavy clothes at home too!

Another reason Santa Rosa Wall attracts so many return visitors is the *wide variety of marine life* consistently found along its cliffs. On a single dive you may encounter barracuda, parrotfish, angelfish, butterflyfish, sand divers, moray eels, stingrays, filefish, sea turtles, blacktip reef sharks, blue tangs, porkfish, triggerfish, puffers, and trunkfish ... to name just a few.

Palancar Gardens: This is perhaps the most famous dive site off Cozumel. The reef is large and requires a few dives to really see all it has to offer. The area referred to as "The Gardens" is made up of a series of tunnels that pass under the reef. Each tunnel is about twenty feet long, and you can always see the entry point and daylight. Swimming through these passages is definitely one of the highlights of diving Cozumel!

Large animals, such as sleeping nurse sharks, will sometimes be encountered in the tunnels ... along with a countless variety of fish. On one dive I saw the largest barracuda I've ever seen — hovering under a rocky ledge.

Paradise Reef: Located almost in front of El President Hotel, Paradise Reef is a shallow dive (about forty feet), often done as a second dive after one of the deeper wall dives.

Paradise Reef may be the best place in the world for fish photography. The variety of species is amazing and the animals show very little fear of divers. Angelfish are the most common and will approach within a foot of your mask.

Unusual species can also be easily found on Paradise Reef. I consistently saw unusual looking *sand divers* at this site. Angelfish approach divers since they are quite accustomed to people and are left unmolested.

As with most dive sites off Cozumel, Paradise Reef is a drift dive. The easiest way to photograph fish is to "drift" with them, taking pictures as you go. Be sure to keep an eye out for the incredibly large, green moray eel that lives on this reef.

When visiting Cozumel, I highly recommend you stay at La Ceiba Hotel, which is a short two-minute cab ride from town and specifically set up for divers. Located right on the water, La Ceiba complex offers a large beach, swimming pool, hot tub, tennis court, workout gym, and sauna ... and all rooms have cable TV via a satellite dish. Keep in mind that this is Mexico; most of the other hotels offer a room — period.

La Ceiba Hotel offers lots of little luxuries that will make your stay in Mexico much more enjoyable. For example, imported bottled water is kept in dispensers on every floor (free of charge). This is nice since a lack of bottled water can ruin your stay in Cozumel. I had some friends traveling with me who didn't stay at La Ceiba ... they got sick from drinking the "purified water" in their hotel and missed a day of diving.

La Ceiba dive shop is located on the beach and has its *own pier and diveboats*. It's an extremely convenient arrangement — you simply walk out of your room and onto the boats. There are lockers a few feet from where the boats depart, so you don't have to carry anything to the boat each day. You sign up the day before for the morning or afternoon boat, and when you arrive the next day for the dive, your gear will be waiting for you on the dock!

Another aspect I really appreciated about La Ceiba operation is the fact they *acknowledge that advanced divers want advanced dives*. I dive with a computer and enjoy deep diving; I also almost always dive a multilevel profile that extends bottom times beyond standard dive tables. The dive shop at La Ceiba arranged a smaller boat for our group and allowed us the freedom to dive the way we wanted. The charge for the private boat is only $10 (U.S.) more than the regular boat. If you are an advanced diver, I highly recommend you go with the smaller boat.

Two angelfish cruise along Paradise Reef.

The reef in front of La Ceiba Hotel is excellent for both snorkelers and divers.

14 | The Coronado Islands

Not all underwater adventures have to be expensive! Sixty foot plus visibility, huge sea lion colonies, purple coral, large populations of game fish, and even an occasional whale are just some of the reasons why many divers often make repeat trips to the Coronado Islands. The fact that you can get there for about $25 from San Diego makes these "foreign" islands extremely affordable!

Located about seven miles off the Mexican shoreline and fifteen miles south of the California/Mexico border, the small group of four islands is a short one-and-one-half-hour boat ride from San Diego Harbor. The four islands that make up the Coronado Islands are referred to as: South Island (1.8 miles long and the biggest), North Island (.8 miles long), and Middle Island and Middle Rock (commonly referred to as "The Middle Ground"). North and South Islands are only about two and one-half miles apart, with the Middle Ground between them. The fact the area is so small makes diving all of the Coronado Islands in a single day feasible. As each island offers something different, a day spent diving Coronado Islands can yield a wide variety of underwater experiences. The purple coral growing on the reef off North Island's South Point is particularly worth visiting.

The Coronado Islands were given their name by Father Antonio de la Ascension, a priest who sighted the islands on November 8, 1602, while sailing on the Vizcaino expedition. He named the islands to commemorate "Los Cuatro Martires Coronados" (the four martyrs), who were killed for their faith in early Rome, and whose holy day was November 8th.

The Coronados Islands are not a part of the community of Coronado located in San Diego. In 1886, when Babcock and Story, the first promoters of mainland Coronado, were looking for a name for their new development, they held a contest and selected Coronado as the winning name.

When traveling to the Coronado Islands, be aware that Mexican law requires that every passenger on a boat entering Mexican waters have a Mexican fishing license. Most commercial diveboats obtain the license for you and include the cost in the charter fee. The license is really a usage permit since one is needed even if you are not fishing. In fact, spearfishing on scuba with pneumatic guns is prohibited, as is the taking of abalone, lobster, scallops, and some other shellfish. To obtain up-to-date information on fish and game regulations in Mexican waters, and to purchase licenses for private boats, contact: The Mexican Department of Fisheries, 2550 5th Avenue, Suite 11, San Diego, CA 92103, (619) 233-6956.

Dive sites around the Coronados are divided into three groups: North Island, South Island, and the Middle Ground.

Lobster Shack: Located along the lee side of North Island, Lobster Shack is probably the most well-known dive site off the Coronado Islands. One reason is the cove's shallow, sandy bottom, which attracts local San Diego-based instructors to Lobster Shack (also called Lobster Cove) to use the area for checkout dives.

The most interesting diving is at the northern end of the cove. A cliff meets the water and continues to drop steeply below the water line, stopping at about twenty feet, where large boulders are scattered along the bottom. The "reputed" lobsters are said to live in the nooks and crannies around the boulders. At about thirty feet, the bottom levels out onto sandy plains. Unfortunately, the sandy bottom is covered with man's debris — I encountered an engine of some type, a lawn chair, a pole spear, two weight belts, numerous beer cans, other trash, and a few lobster traps.

Eel grass can be found growing close to shore in some areas of the cove. Traditionally, "bugs" (as lobsters are sometimes called) have been known to be seen (but not taken) in these areas.

South Point: Located at the southern tip of North Island, this is one of the best areas (conditions permitting) off the Coronado Islands. The area is actually made up of three different sites that are relatively close together.

The area just northwest of the point, slightly south of the archway, is one of the prettiest dives on North Island and is an ideal site for both wide-angle and macro-photography. Large finger reefs run parallel to each other in about seventy-five feet of water and are covered with clusters of purple coral, large sea stars, sea hares, urchins, and other invertebrates. The finger reefs are separated by sandy areas where large bat rays can occasionally be found.

The Archway: Located about seventy-five yards north of South Point, the arch is formed both above and below the water and is big enough for divers to swim through. Passing through the arch takes you from one side of the island to the other, so make sure someone knows where you are headed, since currents in the area can be strong. Leading into the arch from the west side of South Point is "the slot," a slowly narrowing corridor with steep walls covered with strawberry anemones, cup corals, and other colorful invertebrates. Unfortunately, macro-photography in the area is difficult at best due to the strong surge in the area.

Blue Grotto: This dive site is on the eastern side of the Archway and South Point. Although a diver can swim from one side of the island to the other by passing under the arch, a diveboat can't and so must choose to anchor on one side or the other.

The bottom terrain is made up of large boulders typical of much of the Coronado Islands. Spearfisherman (skin diving, not scuba) will do well in this area. On one dive I saw a school of surprisingly large yellowtail. Kelp bass, sheepshead, sculpin, and rockfish are also common.

The Rookery: Located on the seaward side of North Island, The Rookery is often adversely affected by weather, thus rarely dove. However, if you are into swimming with sea lions, this is the place! The cove can be identified by the two "cave-like" hollow spots above the water line … and of course by the numerous sea lions in the area. Chances are, the moment you enter the water you will be joined by a dozen or so sea lions ranging in size from four to ten feet. Obviously, this is an ideal site for photographers and sightseers alike.

Pukey Point: As its name implies, Pukey Point is another site where conditions can be prohibitive to diving. Located at the north end of North Island, Pukey Point is a favorite of spearfisherman. Unusually large yellowtail and tuna have been taken off the point. Blue shark sightings are fairly common … which also attracts photographers into the area.

Sea Lion Cove: Located on the northern side of Middle Island, Sea Lion Cove, as its name implies, is known to be inhabited by numerous sea lions. However, during two separate trips to Sea Lion Cove I didn't see a single sea mammal. Perhaps they have relocated to The Rookery off North Island. The bottom is made of large boulders, some of which rise up fifteen feet from the bottom. Moray eels can be found in the area, and make interesting photo subjects. Macro-photographers will appreciate the nu-

A female sheepshead off the Coronado Islands.

merous tubeworms, anemones, sea stars, sea hares, and tunicates living on the reef.

Moonlight Cove: On the south side of Middle Island, Moonlight Cove is one of the most protected coves around the Coronado Islands. Visibility is slightly better at Moonlight than at Sea Lion Cove, with seventy feet being the average. The flat, sandy bottom in forty feet of water makes Moonlight Cove a favorite of dive instructors conducting open water checkout dives.

Kelp and other forms of underwater vegetation are conspicuously missing from the Coronado Islands. Mexican abalone, lobster, and sea urchin fisherman have cut the kelp away to gain easier access to the reefs. The lack of vegetation creates a "barren" feel to some dive sites around the Coronados. Moonlight Cove, however, is one of the few sites where vegetation can be seen.

The Gap: The area between Middle Island and Middle Rock. Depth is in the thirty- to sixty-foot range — with the bottom made up of a series of finger reefs. The site is an ideal spot for spearfishing since large, open water species often swim through "the gap" on their way to open water. Black sea bass have also been sighted on a few occasions.

The Ridges: Located north of Middle Rock, The Ridges have depths ranging from forty to eighty feet. The Ridges run roughly from North Island to South Island and are also frequented by hunters. Currents in this area, however, can be extremely strong, so caution is advised.

Middle Ground Rock: One of the most photogenic areas in the Middle Ground. The west side of the rock drops off quickly to about seventy feet, where the bottom is made up of large boulders. The numerous moray eels, large sea stars, rounders, anemones, and sea urchins found at the site make it ideal for photography.

Casino Cove: Named after the casino that was built during the Prohibition years to serve "dry" U.S. citizens. Once Prohibition came to an end and alcohol was available in San Diego, the Coronado Islands "resort" status also came to an end. The casino was finally destroyed about four years ago during a storm. The fact that Casino Cove has such a colorful history brings into the area divers seeking unusual artifacts. Old bottles and jars from the 1920s and 1930s are particularly prized finds.

Casino Cove is one of the best anchorages around the Coronados. The generally calm conditions and shallow depths make Casino Cove another site often used by instructors for open water checkout dives.

Puerto Cueva Cove: Located north of Casino Cove on the east side of South Island. Diveboats will often use the site as an alternative if Casino Cove has other boats anchored in it.

North End Rock: Located at the north end of South Island, spearfisherman often hunt the area looking for large animals passing by

Divers dive off the Sand Dollar *at the Coronado Islands.*

"the end" of the island from open water. When boating in the area, keep an eye out for dive flags in the water, since spearfisherman generally tow a float (and dive flag) behind them to place their catch in. The Coronados, and North End Rock in particular, are frequently visited by hunters. One recent Sunday afternoon I counted six small dive flags bobbing along . . . all of which were apparently diving from private boats.

Elephant Seal Cove: Located on the west side of South Island, as its name implies, Elephant Seal Cove is inhabited by elephant seals during the winter. As with many seaward facing sites off the Coronados, conditions at Elephant Seal Cove can be prohibitive to diving.

Jackass Rock: This is an ideal site for photographers and sightseers. Located almost midway down the eastern side of South Island, the area is well-known for the numerous moray eels that are frequently photographed. The shallow depths in the area make Jackass Rock an ideal site for novice divers seeking calm conditions. In addition to the moray eels, Jackass Rock is home to dozens of extremely large sea hares. In fact, sea hares seem to be encountered a lot more often at the Coronado Islands than the California Channel Islands. The sea hares around the Coronado Islands also seem to have a much wider range of color and size than those found off the Channel Islands.

Halibut Flats: As its name implies, Halibut Flats is known to be a good site for halibut. Located on the east side of South Island, the area is another good choice for novice divers due to the shallow depths and generally calm conditions.

South End: Not to be confused with South Point off North Island, South End is the southern end of South Island. Diveboats generally don't visit the area since currents are extremely strong almost year-round.

Although the west side of South Island hasn't been visited by divers much (due to the difficult conditions), it is believed that there are a couple wrecks in the area. If conditions are conducive, exploring this area may reveal some surprising finds.

5 Minute Kelp: Located one and a half miles south of Coronado del Sur, 5 Minute Kelp is a sea mount that rises up to about sixty feet of water. Unfortunately, there currently isn't any kelp at the site since the Mexican fishermen have hacked it all away.

12 Fathom Spot: Located seven miles southeast of Coronado del Sur, 12 Fathom Spot is another open water site. The reef comes within about seventy feet of the surface and features steep drop-offs that plummet as deep as 200 feet. Due to the depths involved, 12 Fathom Spot should only be visited by experienced divers.

The fact that blue sharks are occasionally encountered at 12 Fathom Spot accounts for the many photographers who favor the area. In addition to large pelagics, the rocky reef is also home to numerous species of sculpin, cabezon, croaker, sea bass, lingcod, and rockfish — all of which make interesting photographic subjects.

15 | Moray Eels

"Today you're going to meet Chewy," beamed Lorraine as the twenty-four-foot *Argonaut* slowly pulled out of Avalon harbor. For the last three days Lorraine Sadler had been giving me an underwater tour of the moray eels that she had been working with around the island.

"Does Chewy bite?" I asked curiously. Considering the fact that one large eel had attempted to "chew" on my earlobe a few months ago while Marty Snyderman filmed Lorraine and me feeding the eels for a documentary, I felt my apprehension was justifiable. Actually, the ear-nibbler was merely snapping at exhaust bubbles from my regulator and didn't do any damage to me at all.

"Don't be silly," Lorraine smiled. "You know moray eels don't bite people." She was right. Moray eels have one of the most undeserved reputations in the animal kingdom. Believed by many to be vicious, snake-like creatures, eager to lunge at their prey and impale them with their fang-like teeth, moray eels are feared by much of the general public.

The truth is that these animals are extremely docile and are of no threat to divers. The only time people get bitten is when they inadvertently stick their hand in a hole where a moray eel lives (usually to grab a lobster). One of the most ridiculous stories is that a moray eel can't open its mouth once it bites into something unless it first closes it all the way. Wide-eyed novice divers are told that the eel must be brought to the surface where the jaws are "pried" off! This is completely untrue. I've seen dozens of eels bite into objects that were too big, only to let go when they realized they were incapable of tearing a chunk off. One of the most interesting behaviors the eels exhibit is "corkscrewing," or spinning rapidly while biting into something to tear it loose. The speed at which they do this is amazing.

"Let's go diving!" exclaimed an enthusiastic Lorraine ... moments before we rolled into the water. Watching Lorraine "dance" with her eels is an experience I always look forward to. We swam through the kelp bed and slowly approached the reef where two large eels swam out to greet us. Fortunately, Lorraine's eels are at dive sites only known to her. It would be sad, I thought, if these animals swam out to greet spear-carrying divers.

As I settled on the bottom and took a light-reading of the open water behind Lorraine, she began her well-practiced routine of enticing the eels into her arms with chunks of abalone. Seeing a large moray as thick as a man's thigh allowing itself to be gently handled makes one realize how non-threatening these animals are. Suddenly, the smaller eel bolted behind me with frightening speed. I turned around in time to see the tentacles of a small octopus go down its throat. This happening during the day was truly amazing since octopi are generally nocturnal creatures.

California moray eels (Family: *Muraenidae*) are really fish; they reach an average length of about six feet and are nocturnal feeders. They breathe by sucking water through their mouths and out their gills. To accomplish this, the animals are constantly opening and closing their mouths, which contributes to people interpreting them as "eager" to attack. They feed primarily on octopi, abalone, and small fish. Lorraine showed me an amazing tape of a moray eel smashing an abalone against a rock.

Tropical moray eels come in a wider range of sizes and colors. In Cozumel's Paradise Reef lives a gigantic green moray that must be seen to be believed! Palau is home to some of the world's most colorful species of small eels.

Lorraine Sadler handles one of her moray eels.

16 | An Eel Story

"They taste like lobster," explained Jon as the group of fourteen-year-old boys rowed their small boat out to the reef. The year was 1960 and the group was planning to spear a moray eel that would be eaten for dinner that night.

"How long will we need to stay down?" asked one of the teenagers.

"Not more than thirty seconds or so," replied Jon.

Once the group arrived at their intended destination, Jon entered the water to spear an eel and took one of the boys with him. It should be noted that their "attitude" towards spearfishing was notably different.

Within moments of dropping below the water line, the pair of skin-divers spotted a large animal that would easily feed the entire group. Instinctively, Jon let his pole spear fly and captured the animal.

"He got it ... he got it!" yelled Jon's companion as the two of them surfaced. Not wanting the eel to get away, Jon tossed the animal in the back of the boat. What he hadn't planned on was the boys' terrified reaction to the eel, which was by no means dead, and started flopping around! To get away from the "monster," the boys all crowded at the boat's bow ... which swamped the ship with water and caused it to begin sinking. The eel, which now had water to swim in, immediately commandeered the flooded craft.

"Head for shore!" screamed one of the boys as they all abandoned ship.

Taking command of the situation to prevent the youngsters from injuring themselves, Jon instructed them to swim the boat in while singing sailor songs. With the added weight of the water (not to mention the eel happily swimming around inside the boat), it took them almost an hour to reach shore.

Later that night, the youngsters enjoyed "hero" status as their group sat around the campfire eating roasted moray eel.

17 | Ralph White

Ralph White has logged more bottom time on the *Titanic* than any other American. In fact, he has made more dives than the entire 1986 American expedition to the *Titanic* together. *Titanic* is only one of the over four hundred projects Ralph has worked on.

His résumé reads like a guide to underwater adventure. Photographing the *Breadalbane* required diving 350 feet below Arctic ice. Searching for the fabled Loch Ness monster, Ralph spent three months in near zero visibility. His work on *National Geographic's* "The Great Whales" won him an Emmy.

He has been in the water with piranha, saltwater crocodiles, great white sharks, and killer whales. Often working at depths in the 4,000- to 20,000-foot range, Ralph has had experience with almost every type of submersible vehicle made.

First Dives

Born in San Bernardino, California in 1941, Mr. White is a trim fifty-one years old. In 1945 his father relocated the family to Hawaii, where Ralph grew up. Ralph first learned to skin-dive when a friend gave him a pair of crude goggles. "They were made of bamboo, with glass glued to them. I remember when I got down deep, the goggles pressed into my eyes. It hurt so badly, if you can imagine this dried bamboo pressing into your eye sockets."

In 1955, Ralph logged his first scuba dive with a family friend, Joe Crawford. Armed with a set of triples and a double hose regulator, Ralph spent most of his spare time underwater. "Sometimes those triple tanks would get so buoyant, I would literally put rocks in my shirt and shorts. Occasionally the rocks would be covered with stinging coral and I would get these terrible rashes. Basically, I was fourteen and not using my brain. I'm lucky I didn't kill myself on those early dives."

In 1961, at age twenty, Ralph joined the Marines. As part of the elite Marine Force Recon, he became a military diver. After the military, Ralph found work at North American Aviation.

For recreational purposes, Ralph took up training as a glider pilot. When the wing fell off the airplane during his seventh hour of training, Ralph discovered skydiving. He has since logged 2,997 jumps.

Wanting to share his skydiving experiences, Ralph began inventing helmet-mounted cameras, wrist-mounted cameras, and other photographic gadgets. Naturally, it wasn't long before an underwater housing was also built. Everything had to be built from scratch. "The problems with taking a camera underwater were ten times more complicated back then. My first camera housing leaked so many times, I almost gave up."

While working at the motion picture lab of the North American Aviation flight test facility, Ralph came across an inner company memorandum. Dr. Andy Rechnipzer was looking for a diver/photographer who could take pictures of his new submersible, the Beaver Mark IV. Fresh out of the military and with lots of underwater time with a camera, Ralph got the job. He's been working ever since.

Loch Ness

In 1976 Ralph went to Scotland in search of the Loch Ness monster. Using sonar-triggered cameras and underwater baiting techniques, he filmed some large eels. The biggest eel seen was ten feet in length, long enough to be called a monster.

They also found some high concentrations of Arctic char. Since no one had seen an Arctic char since the mid-1940s, the local game wardens didn't believe it until Ralph and David Doubilet went down and documented it.

The lakes around Loch Ness are a breeding ground for huge salmon. The salmon were the biggest problem encountered while diving Loch Ness. "David Doubilet, Emory Kristof, and I were diving, and a school of salmon just went through us, knocked our masks off, pulled the cameras out of our hands — it was a real mess."

Divers on the Loch Ness expedition were supplied with dry suits. Unfortunately, most of the photographers had never used one. Emory Kristof designed some custom weights to go with the new dry suits. "On Emory's first dive, he released the air from his suit and sunk so fast his fins folded up parallel to his shins. We had to pull him out of about a foot of mud. It's lucky we saw him sink because the suction was really preventing him from getting out."

Dangerous Times

Ralph once found himself in the middle of an out-of-control, gray reef shark feeding frenzy. It was due to overzealous baiting. "I knew we were in trouble when one of the sharks made a direct run at John Bird and cracked his face plate. It cut him up pretty bad. We had expended all our bang sticks because they were really getting aggressive. We had to take cover and wait it out."

Ralph's most concerned moment was off San Clemente Island when Valerie Taylor got raked across the calf by a blue shark. While Howard Hall and Marty Snyderman helped her out of the water, Ralph called the Coast Guard to send for a helicopter. He also called Jennifer Carter, who had had

Although pretty to look at, this stinging soft coral can be painful if touched.

the same thing happen to her with a tiger. Jennifer arranged for a plastic surgeon to meet Valerie.

On another dive, Ralph's tank valve sheared off in eighty feet of water. Ralph found himself so negatively buoyant, he couldn't ascend. This was due to his scuba tank filling up with water. He was sinking, without an air supply, and with a very expensive 35mm movie camera in his hands. The other divers in the water just froze — no one came to his assistance.

Howard Hall was standing on the deck of the boat. When he saw that Ralph was in trouble, he free-dove down, without the assistance of a mask or fins, and took the camera from Ralph. "He wanted to help me, but I pushed the camera into his arms." Freed from the burden of the camera, Ralph ditched his tank and weights and made an ascent. "I credit Howard Hall with saving my life that day."

A Thirty-Foot Shark

Ralph's latest discovery is a thirty-foot carnivorous shark in 4,000 feet of water off Japan. To attract these large animals, a cage filled with tuna is placed on the bottom. It's then a matter of waiting inside the submersible to see what shows up. "The French crew [who owned the sub] thought we were a little bizarre to want to use a $30,000-a-day submersible to bait sharks. They said: 'You know, we can bait sharks right off the fantail, why do you want to use the submersible?' Of course after the first dive their energy level was way up."

When the shark showed up one of the crew yelled, "We got a whale down here." Ralph looked out the porthole and realized it wasn't a whale from the texture of its skin. "I didn't know what it was, but I knew to roll all cameras." What followed was an exciting few moments as the animal pushed a 30,000 pound sub around. "At this point we still didn't know what it was because we couldn't see the entire animal."

It wasn't until the animal's head came into view that Ralph recognized it as a Pacific shark (*Somniosus pacificus*). "The problem with photographing large animals in deep water is there's usually not a point of reference to judge their size by. Fortunately, I got footage of the shark by our bait cage. It's thirty feet long, and not a plankton eater."

On the same dive, Ralph shot footage of an extremely large deep water shark eating another shark of about the same size. It is unique because the shark is swallowing it snake style, head first, and in one piece. "As far as I know, this is the first time anything like this has been seen."

Piranha

An assignment to film a piranha feeding frenzy presented some challenges. Because visibility in the Amazon River is close to zero, it was decided to film the piranha in a specially constructed tank. To avoid being bitten, Ralph built an acrylic sphere. This enabled him to film in all directions without any obstructions, and still be protected. Since the sphere was sealed, using scuba was ruled out because of the exhaust bubbles. Ralph's solution was to use an oxygen re-breather.

Another device used to film piranha was a piece of PVC pipe with an acrylic dome bolted on each end. Ralph would lie inside the pipe and film through the dome. Once again, the re-breather had to be used to avoid making bubbles.

The Titanic

Ralph's proudest accomplishment (to date) is his involvement with the *Titanic*. "When I used to think about the *Titanic*, I never conceived in my mind the possibility of ever being able to dive it. So to be able to dive on it, and run the kind of operation we ran in 1987, was probably the greatest thrill of my life."

Ralph is one of the few people to have participated in both the 1985 French/American expedition and the 1987 French expedition. He is currently talking to the Russians about the possibility of returning to the *Titanic*. One of the most dramatic moments of Ralph's career was his first dive on the *Titanic*. "I was watching the sector scanning sonar, so I knew when to really focus attention. It was really dramatic the way the bow suddenly loomed up."

One of the problems with working at *Titanic's* depth of 12,558 feet is the cold. Heaters aren't used due to the risk of fire, and the temperature inside the sub drops to 2 degrees Centigrade. With dives often lasting over ten hours, observers would get terrible headaches from having their foreheads pressed up against the sub's freezing cold porthole. Bladder control also became extremely important.

A World Record

Ralph was a member of the Soviet/American team that set the world record for the deepest submersible rendezvous. The submersibles used were the Russian-built MIR I and MIR II. Constructed in 1987 by Ramo-Repolla in Finland at a cost of $40,000,000, the MIR subs represent state-of-the-art in deep submersible technology. MIR translated means "peace."

On June 22, 1989, MIR I was launched from the Soviet support vessel *Keldysh*. An hour later, with Ralph aboard, MIR II was also launched. "The reason for the hour separation was to avoid a possible collision between the two subs in the water column. In the three and a half hours it takes us to descend to the bottom, we are virtually a falling brick without power."

Because MIR I landed in a gully, it took the two subs four hours to locate each other. When they did, at 16,500 feet, the record was set. Only a handful of explorers have ever attained this depth.

Other Accomplishments

The list of Ralph White's accomplishments is endless. Ralph was project director on Operation Phoenix, which involved the discovery and recovery of numerous Spanish galleons.

He was the first cinematographer to shoot footage of divers swimming with blue whales. Ralph has worked extensively with grey whales, filming their annual migration from the Bering Sea to Scammon's Lagoon. In appreciation for his contributions, the promontory point above the nursery channel Punto Rudolpho is named after him.

As a member of the Aegir Habitat team, Ralph spent over a week living below 500 feet. With such a vast array of experience to choose from, one might wonder what Ralph's most memorable adventure was. When asked, he enthusiastically replied: "I hope I haven't done it yet!"

18 | Palau

"Forget about swimming," Dennis was explaining, as Christine and Samantha geared up for a dive in *Wonder Channel*, off the islands of Palau. "The currents are too strong to fight," Dennis continued.

"Why are they any stronger than the currents on the wall dives we've been making all week?" asked Samantha.

"This is different," said Dennis. "The channel was created by blasting through miles of coral heads to create a safe passage for boats. When the tide changes, the channel acts like a giant siphon as water is sucked through at great speed."

I was listening to this exchange with amusement, thinking to myself, "Yeah, yeah, I've heard all this before at other sites that supposedly had strong currents." Little did I know ...

As usual, I threw my tank, B.C., and regulator into the water just before jumping in, since I've always found it easier to put my tank on in the water. Seconds after entering the water, the tank was on my back. To my utter amazement, I had also drifted over one hundred feet from the boat ... and yes, swimming against this current was absolutely impossible. The only logical thing to do was to drop down, get into the "mainstream" of the channel, and enjoy the ride!

Once on the bottom, the importance of buoyancy control immediately became apparent. Getting slammed into a pile of coral at this speed could definitely result in a pair of "shredded" legs. Taking pictures was also completely out of the question.

After a few minutes, I spotted a large clump of dead coral and decided to hang on to see if Christine and Samantha were behind me. Just as my hand was torn free, I spotted Samantha and Christine zooming towards me at amazing speed.

The three of us spent the next twenty minutes rocketing through the channel, gently steering ourselves with minor fin movements. Of all the dive sites in the world, Wonder Channel is definitely one place you shouldn't miss.

Located in the south Pacific, the ninety-three-mile chain of 320 islands that make up Palau offers divers what may be the most spectacular diving in the world — two hundred foot plus visibility, 86 degree water, and an amazingly wide variety of marine life. You can almost be guaranteed of seeing sharks on every dive, along with giant circular corals over fifteen feet in diameter.

Colorful crinoids are often seen in the South Pacific.

In addition to Wonder Channel, another excellent site off Palau is the *Blue Holes*. The holes drop down ninety feet or so through a barrier reef and then dump you out along a wall. Sitting at the bottom of one of these tunnels while divers "rain down" from above is something most people remember for some time.

Wall dives off Palau, such as *Ngemelis*, are without doubt some of the most spectacular in the world. Gigantic blood red Gorgonians, crinoids, beautiful reef fish, sharks, massive schools of barracuda — all these await the adventurous diver.

One thing to keep in mind is that it is dangerously easy to wander into deep water off Palau. Our dive guide, Dennis, for example, routinely dropped down to 200 feet, where he and his pals would float while enjoying the sensation of being "narced" to oblivion. When I asked him if he used a computer, he indignantly held up his wrist watch and stated, "Nitrogen ... scared of Dennis." Two days later, when he bent himself (for the fifth time, he proudly told me), the other dive guides congratulated him on his bravery. The moral of the story is that while Palau is one of the most beautiful destinations for scuba diving, you must take responsibility for your own safety (this applies anywhere you go).

Huge circular corals, such as the one Christine is examining here, are common off Palau.

19 | Bonaire

Located sixty-six miles off the coast of Venezuela, Bonaire has long been recognized as one of the top scuba diving destinations in the world. Of all the places I've been, this is the only island where the beach diving was truly as enjoyable as the boat dives. In fact, the reef in front of Captain Don's Habitat is one of my favorite locations for underwater photography in the world (perhaps because I've sold numerous cover shots from this reef). If you are looking for a versatile underwater tropical location, combined with nearby first-class accommodations ... I highly recommend this resort.

Bonaire, and its two sister islands Aruba and Curacao (commonly referred to as the ABC islands), were first "discovered" by the Spanish in 1499. In the 1600s, Holland established a settlement on Curacao, where salt mining operations were started. Salt mining rapidly became the island's main source of revenue, with Bonaire producing the greatest output. Although the salt mines on Bonaire are still operational, tourism supplies much of its revenue.

Water temperature is an average of 78 degrees year-round and visibility is often well over one hundred feet. Underwater terrain off Bonaire consists mostly of a gently sloping bottom along with an occasional wall dive. Some of the most beautiful dive sites around the island are:

Rappel: Probably the most well-known dive off Bonaire, this spectacular wall is known for the large branches of rarely seen black coral often photographed here. Large schools of tarpon are occasionally seen cruising along the wall, as are barracuda and numerous colorful reef fish. Photographers and sightseers will want to make more than one dive to see the entire area. This is an excellent spot for night diving.

Munk's Haven: Located off Klein Bonaire, the huge clusters of elkhorn coral are what bring divers to Munk's Haven. As with many sites around Bonaire, Munk's Haven is decorated with large purple tube sponges that rise several feet towards the surface. Various colorful species of angelfish swim lazily along the bottom, supplying photographers with cooperative subjects. Keep an eye out for the small spotted moray eels that live in the numerous crevices in the area.

Bari Reef: If you stay at the excellent Sand Dollar Resort, you will most likely make your first dive at Bari Reef, which is located just offshore. The bottom slopes gently from the surface to about 130 feet (typical of most of the island's beach dives) and feels like a big aquarium. Countless small tropical fish dart around the coral heads and are relatively fearless of

Bonaire offers vacationers world-class diving.

divers, since the area is basically dove all day. Bari Reef is a terrific spot for night diving due to its easy access and prolific marine life.

Playa Benge: Located in the Washington-Slagbaai National Park, Playa Benge offers divers a combination of steep drop-offs decorated with a wide selection of coral species, large marine life, great visibility, and generally calm conditions. Keep an eye out for schools of squid if you make a night dive here.

Captain Don's Habitat: The reef in front of the resort's dive center is well worth a visit. The reef slopes gently from the surface to 130 feet, where a sandy bottom begins and a mid-size wreck provides photo opportunities. Another small wreck lies capsized in sixty feet and is home to a large grouper, who often allows divers to pet him. A rope lies along the bottom (put there by the resort) to guide divers from the dock to the wreck in 130 feet. This makes navigation and orientation in the area easy since you are always either at a left or right angle to the rope (providing you remember). All divers have to do is swim at a right angle to the sloping bottom until they return to the guideline ... and then to shore. The line also makes holding your position during decompression and safety stops easy.

20 | Aruba

Of all the ABC islands, Aruba is the best choice if you travel with non-diving family members or friends who wish to participate in "topside" activities while you pursue new underwater adventures. Perhaps you can entice them to accompany you to Aruba by telling them that gold was discovered in its mountains in 1824 and the mines are still open to tourists. Of the three ABC islands, Aruba has the widest variety of stores, restaurants, and other facilities.

The wreck of the *Antilla*, which was scuttled by its German crew during World War II, is one of the most popular wreck dives in the islands. Your non-diving companions may choose to observe your underwater adventures from the safety of the *Atlantis* submarine, which conducts underwater tours of the wreck and other sites off Aruba.

Located on the southeastern tip of the island, the area known as *Baby Beach* is an excellent beach dive. Huge branches of elkhorn coral can be seen practically everywhere. Photographers and sightseers may want to spend some time looking for the colorful fish that hide in the safety of the elkhorn's branches.

It is commendable that the dive operators of these islands have placed moorings at practically all the dive sites. The moorings prevent damage to the reefs since the boats don't have to drop anchor; they merely tie up to the mooring.

Aruba, with its miles of beautiful beaches, is often used for calendar shots.

An unusual-looking lizardfish.

21 | Curacao

The wreck of the *Superior Producer* may be the most beautiful wreck in the Caribbean, and is only one of the countless reasons that Curacao rates high on any list of great underwater adventures.

The island is much more rugged in appearance than the nearby sister islands of Bonaire and Aruba. The main town of Willemstad, with a population of 250,000, is the island's main hub of activity and also houses the oldest operating synagogue in the western hemisphere (founded in 1651; built in 1732). Another interesting sight is the old Dutch Fort that once provided protection for islanders against Caribbean pirates. Captain Bligh is said to have led a raid against the town.

The attitude is extremely laid back and carefree, exemplified by the fact that nudity is not uncommon on some of the island's public beaches. If you are looking to combine underwater adventures with some peaceful on-shore relaxation, then this Dutch community may be exactly what you're looking for.

An interesting site is the "floating bridge" at the harbor's entrance; it's the only one in the western hemisphere. After a visit to the bridge, you may wish to sample some of Curacao's excellent restaurants, which serve up a delicious variety of international cuisines.

Klein Curacao is an island that lies off the east end of Curacao. Although excellent diving and shore exploration exist, the island lacks natural fresh water, so there aren't any "resorts" there. However, divers — especially macro-photographers — flock to this island due to the seemingly endless variety of subjects that are everywhere! Over a dozen different species of shrimp can be found hiding amongst the numerous and colorful sea anemones that decorate the bottom. Large pelagics are often encountered swimming along the deeper sections of the wall. Elephant ear sponges, Gorgonians, and (of course) purple tube sponges await the wide-angle photographer; this is an excellent spot for diver pictures.

The unique-looking frogfish is a prize discovery for both photographers and sightseers, but is hard to locate due to its excellent camouflage.

One of the nice things about Curacao is that there are a lot of dive sites waiting to be discovered. While Bonaire's underwater environment has been extensively explored, Curacao's has not.

22 | Fire Divers

I recently had the opportunity to meet a group of people who may be the most adventurous divers of all!

This unique branch of the fire department began in 1959 when a young rookie stopped by Station House 49 of the San Pedro, California Fire Department to visit his coworkers on his day off. As he walked into the fire station, he had no way of knowing that the next few hours of his life would mark the beginning of one of the most extraordinary chapters in fire department history!

As soon as Claude Creasey got out of his car, he could tell something *big* was going on. "There's a fire at Matson Terminal!" yelled a fellow rookie through the commotion of men running to their stations. Reacting more on instinct than thought, Creasey dropped his jacket and raced for the *fireboat*.

The fire had been started by somebody who was welding a crane. By the time the fireboat arrived on the scene, a couple hundred feet of the wharf was ablaze. Because of the size of the incident, the firemen found themselves face to face with one of the largest fires in the harbor's history without the guidance of a chief to direct them! The quick-thinking Creasey immediately took charge and began to direct streams of water under the dock in an attempt to control the fire.

After two hours of scorching firefighting, very little progress had been made. One of the main problems was the fact that the fireboats couldn't get under the docks due to the low ceilings and because the pier pilings were so close together. In an attempt to resolve the problem, a few firemen jumped into the water and swam the hose under the dock.

The next morning, Claude Creasey was summoned to the office of Assistant Chief W.W. Johnson. Since Assistant Chiefs didn't talk to rookies unless they were in some kind of trouble, Creasey thought he was going to be reprimanded for his presumptuous behavior during the Matson Terminal fire. When he arrived at his superior's office, he was pleasantly surprised.

W.W. Johnson was impressed by the way Claude Creasey and the other firemen on his boat had taken command during the previous day's fire! He wanted to know what Creasey thought about the possibility of using scuba divers to fight fires in the water. W.W. Johnson and his son were both divers, as was Creasey.

Claude Creasey is still seeing action at Station 49 in San Pedro ... except he is no longer a rookie. Today he is *Chief* Claude Creasey and still oversees the dive program.

Forty-five-year-old Captain Gary Clark is the scuba coordinator for the current Specialty Firefighting Unit. The unit is made up of eighteen active divers and has three thirty-four-foot firefighting diveboats. In most incidents, each boat carries two divers. If additional manpower is needed, all eighteen divers can be called in. There are also six divers who are maintained as a "reserve" ... so in a maximum commitment situation, Captain Clark may have twenty-four divers in the water!

Captain Gary Clark and the rest of the firemen at Station 49 were kind enough to give me a demonstration of how their unit operates. Captain Clark was joined in the water by fellow divers Gary Smith, Dave Fair, and Gary Cline.

The Scuba Unit works in conjunction with the larger firefighting ships. When a call is received, the large firefighting ships, fire trucks, and diveboats all leave for the scene. Usually the boats get there first since the waterways are generally a more direct route. The divers get into their wet suits as they travel to the fire, but they may find that they are needed as *land-based* firefighters once they arrive on the scene.

When they arrive at the fire, the large ships move as close to the site as possible and dump the large floats that support the fire hoses and nozzles. As soon as the floats hit the water, the diveboats move in and deposit the divers. The divers' first job is to maneuver the floats into position under the wharf. They must also attach the feed lines to the pumps located on-board the diveboats.

Two types of *hose floats* are used. One resembles a large sprinkler and sprays water straight up into the air. These are used under piers and can be left unmanned if need be. Another type of float supplies enough flotation to the hose nozzle so the divers don't have to hold it up. These allow the divers to direct the streams of water anywhere they wish.

One of the major hazards to the divers comes from the material that is used as a protective coating on the pier pilings. Creosote melts and becomes a molten gooey substance that continues to burn even when it hits the water. When these dripping fireballs come into contact with neoprene wet suits, they burn right through to the divers' flesh!

Support from the large fireboats is important to the divers' safety. While the divers fight the fire in close quarters, the large fireboats move in and blast streams of water from the large, deck-mounted water guns.

Amazingly, these firefighting divers are using conventional sport diving equipment! Captain Clark tells me the wet suits are one of the main problems, since they offer little protection from burning chemicals in the water. Imagine having an irritating, or possibly burning, chemical seep between your skin and wet suit! Another problem is *hypothermia*. During a large scale fire, the divers might be in the water for three or four hours. For these reasons, the divers are currently considering switching to Viking dry suits. It may even be possible to treat the dry suits with a protectant that would prevent holes being burned in the suits.

Another major problem for the divers is *communication*. Captain Clark currently uses a standard walkie-talkie, which he puts in a waterproof bag tethered to his wrist. The walkie-talkie enables him to talk with the boats but not to the other divers. This arrangement is less than ideal since it is not uncommon for Captain Clark and his men to work in zero visibility. On a search and recovery mission deep inside a sunken wreck, it is virtually impossible for the divers to work in unison since they have no way of knowing what the other team members are doing.

To resolve this problem, Captain Clark hopes to receive the budget to purchase full face masks with built-in communication. The Aquacom XO-26 mask and the SSB-2000 receiver/transmitter, both made by OTS Systems, will give the divers in-water communication up to 1,000 yards. If the Scuba Unit receives these masks and uses them with full dry suits, two of their biggest equipment problems will be resolved.

To become a member of this elite branch of Los Angeles City's Fire Department, you must first serve as a (non-diving) fireman for a minimum of three years. After three years, you may apply to the Specialty Scuba Unit. Some of the divers also have experience in other specialty units of the fire department, such as the Hazmat (hazardous material) and Helicopter Units.

Before you will be allowed to come on as a diver, you will have to pass a practical written exam, take an extensive swimming test, which includes a 500-yard swim, and undergo the unit's thorough scuba training program. To help maintain the unit's high standards, divers are required to get re-certified once a year.

Obviously, all firemen have to be in excellent physical shape, and this is especially true for members of the Specialty Scuba Unit. As Captain Clark explains, "During the SP Slip fire a few years ago, we had six seventy-foot fishing boats burning—some of them adrift—and a couple hundred feet of wharf on fire. The divers are in the water for a couple of hours and become physically drained ... at times like that it feels like the whole world's on fire!"

These guys don't just fight fires—even the non-firefighting duties the divers perform require dive skills beyond the range of the average sport diver.

About six months ago, a fisherman was drowning by the Henry Ford Bridge in L.A. Harbor. Fireboat 3 and two of its divers responded to the call and found that the man had sunk to the bottom. Realizing that speed was critical if the man was to be revived, the divers entered the water immediately. The visibility in this section of the harbor is zero—you can't see your hand in front of your face. To locate the man, the divers used a circular

A firefighting diver aims his hose under the wharf.

search pattern. One diver descended with a weighted line and held his position while a second diver swam in a circle around him while holding the other end of the line. After each circle the stationary diver lets out three more feet of line, increasing the size of the search area. The diver who is searching operates entirely by feel.

Fortunately the fisherman was recovered by the divers and revived! Many of the firemen told me that saving a life is the most rewarding aspect of their job.

On another occasion, one of the large cranes that is used to unload the cargo ships fell into the harbor with the operator on-board! These cranes are over one hundred feet tall and have hundreds of feet of steel cable running through them. The Scuba Unit was sent immediately to the site to rescue the unfortunate crane operator. This dive in fifty feet of water, in zero visibility with twisted steel and cables everywhere, was one of the most dangerous dives the unit has made. Sadly, they were unable to reach the crane operator in time.

The firemen at Station 49 enjoy working the harbor beat. As Captain Clark explains: "If you're working uptown, it's physically demanding, after thirty years you're ready to retire and take your pension. Down here we have less fires, but when we do ... they're horrible. Overall, though, this is a terrific place to work."

Engineer Bill Czernik, with thirty-two years on the job, still enjoys being a fireman. Engineer Hughes has been a firemen for thirty-seven years and has no plans for retirement.

So what is it about being a firemen that makes men stay at it for thirty plus years? Captain Gary Clark summarized it for me: "What other job is there where you can have this kind of adventure and get paid for it!"

23 | Dolphin Dives

"Put tuna in the water ... it'll attract anything in the water column." I was talking to Ralph White of the *Titanic* Expedition about my frustrations in trying to entice Pacific white-sided dolphins to play with skin divers in open water.

"If the dolphins do stop, you must entertain them," Ralph continued. "The only reason they'll stick around is to satisfy their curiosity ... do flips, yell at them under water, swim and wave your hands around ... do anything you can to keep their interest!"

After three hours of dolphin-less cruising in open water, we had finally spotted a large school of hundreds of individuals and were on a course that would deliver our boat a few hundred feet in front of their direction of travel.

"Has it occurred to anybody," asked Andrew, "that dumping a marlin head and a bunch of frozen tuna in the water is probably an excellent way to attract a great white shark?"

"Could be," I said, exchanging a humorous look with Jon. Actually, I had spent a few hours the night before wondering about the sanity of Ralph's advice. He did, after all, warn me to look out for sharks ... and his phrase, "attract anything in the water column" kept running through my head.

"Okay," yelled Jon, as he threw the mesh bag containing the marlin head and the tuna in the water. "Go for it."

Jon had stopped the boat about one hundred yards in front of the approaching dolphins, the bait was in the water, and it was time to test Ralph's theory. Scuba gear wasn't needed and would also slow us down should we get the opportunity to swim with the dolphins.

Once in the water we anxiously waited as the animals drew closer. "I think I just saw a mako jump," yelled Jon. "Do you want to get back on the boat?"

"No, let's see if we can get some pictures first," I replied, trying to sound confident and self-assured. Actually, getting back on the boat was beginning to sound like an excellent idea! Before I could respond in the affirmative, we were suddenly surrounded by dolphins. Jon later commented how amazing it was to see the animals actually jump over the people in the water, who were oblivious to what was going on because they were watching other dolphins in front of them. Every time we reached out to touch an individual, the animal somehow managed to keep an inch out of reach.

"Ah ... Paul," exclaimed Chipper, who was in the water a few feet from me, "that's not a dolphin." He was pointing to a large mako shark that was coming towards us at a frightening speed. Our awe of the dolphins was instantly replaced with a healthy dose of fear. Marty Snyderman's words of advice suddenly came to mind: "If you've put bait in the water, and you're in the water when the sharks show up ... it's for real. You had better be prepared to take whatever action may be necessary to protect your life." Getting out of the water now definitely seemed like a good idea!

Before we had time to wave the boat over, the shark blasted past us, almost close enough to touch (although I decided not to attempt it) ... and was gone as quickly as it had appeared. Unfortunately, so were the dolphins.

Diving with dolphins in the Caribbean is a lot easier, since the animals are often attracted to the boat's wake and tend to "stick around" without much incentive. The Caribbean also has the added advantage of warm water and the fact that the dolphin encounters often take place in shallow water.

A diver relaxes on-board the Salty Saddle, *my personal favorite diveboat, in Avalon Harbor.*

24 | Grand Turk

Located at the southern end of the Bahamas chain, Grand Turk Island lies approximately 575 miles southeast of Miami and is just a ninety-minute flight away. If you are looking for world-class diving set in a laid-back, Dutch-like atmosphere, then Grand Turk may be exactly what you're looking for. Year-round temperatures here rarely drop below 70 degrees, with 85 being the average. Water temperatures average 75 degrees in the winter and 80 in the summer. Wall diving is the primary activity and big animals are common!

Lucayan Indians were the first inhabitants of the islands, as has been documented by villages excavated by the University of Illinois during the 1970s. Recent evidence suggests that Grand Turk may have been the first landfall discovered by Columbus rather than San Salvador. In his log book of 1492, Columbus's description of Guanahani is said to describe Hawk's Nest Anchorage much more accurately than any harbor in San Salvador. Another early visitor to the islands was Ponce de León, who visited the island in 1512 during his quest for the legendary Fountain of Youth.

Numerous Spanish ships landed on the island during the early 1500s. In fact, an account from 1540 reports of finding only "one old man" living on the island, which led to the island being named *Isla De El Viejo*, meaning "Old Man Island." The name "Turk" comes from the numerous Turk's head cactus, which resembles the Turkish fez (a round, flat-top hat).

The 1600s brought salt traders to the island, who were attracted to natural salt lakes in the area. Up until the mid-1970s, the salt trade continued to be the island's primary source of revenue. The islands are currently supported entirely by tourism.

The capital of the seven-by-three-mile island is Cockburn Town with a year-round population of 3,700. Numerous shops, hotels, and restaurants cater to an international tourist trade.

Ninety percent of the diving on Grand Turk takes place along the five-mile wall located 300 yards off Turk's western shoreline. There are nineteen moorings located along the wall, each offering different depths, bottom profiles, and variety of green life. Some of the "must see" sights are:

McDonald's: Located under buoy #4, this is said to be one of the best dive sights off the island. Underwater photographers should bring a wide-angle setup and be prepared for numerous loggerhead turtle encounters. This is a good sight for intermediate divers, since depths are in the sixty-to thirty-foot range, although there is a deep wall nearby for the more experienced.

Black Forest: Also known as "the undercut," due to the fact that the wall undercuts and creates a slight overhead ledge. Depth under the buoy (#8) is fifty feet, with the wall dropping down well over one hundred feet. This is a sight for macro-photographers, especially at night. Numerous sponges, corals, tubeworms, and other subjects are abundant. This is a good site to plan a late afternoon dive, followed by a night dive.

Coral Gardens: Located at buoy #12, as its name implies, Coral Gardens is known for the numerous species of coral living here. Depth under the buoy is about thirty-five feet and then drops down in a series of ledges to the wall that begins in about one hundred feet of water. The dive offers something for all levels of ability, as novice divers can spend time in the shallower depths, while experienced divers can explore the deeper sections of the wall.

English Point: Located at buoy #14, this is known for the nine-foot-tall column of star coral that can be found at 110 feet. Manta rays have been photographed in the area, as have large schools of barracuda and an occasional reef shark. This is another sight that makes an excellent night dive, due to the basket stars that "bloom" after dark. Macro-photographers will also enjoy photographing the numerous species of fish that can be found swimming through the coral.

The atmosphere in Grand Turk is extremely relaxed.

25 | Providenciales

Commonly referred to as Provo, Providenciales is rapidly becoming the new hot destination for the international jet set. With a year-round population of 5,000, the thirty-seven-and-one-half square mile island is also becoming well-known for the income-tax-free banking services.

First inhabited by Tiano Indians who lived in the caves at Long Point, as has been evidenced by cave etchings in the area, Provo is home to the oldest known shipwreck in the western hemisphere. Believed to have sunk in 1510, the ship went down on Molasses Reef off the area known as Blue Hills.

John Petty immigrated to the island in 1790 and was awarded 800 acres of land for services rendered to the Crown. For reasons unknown, John Petty and the other loyalists' cotton and sugar plantations failed to turn a profit. Visiting tourists can still see the ruins of those early settlements.

Diving in Provo is similar in profile to nearby Turk, with most diving taking place off the northwestern shore on what may be one of the world's best wall dives. Peak season is May through July, as visibility can be down during winter. Some of the must-see sights are:

Shark Hotel: Like most dive sights around the world with "shark" in the name, it's unlikely you will actually see a shark while diving here. The bottom profile is a series of ledges that start in forty feet of water, where large pillar corals will be encountered. A small wall drops down to ninety feet, where numerous wide-angle photo subjects can be found. Divers working with computers may wish to drop down to the next ledge; caution should be exercised, however, since currents can be strong, and the depth appears to be "bottomless."

The Forest: This area is known for the large basket and barrel sponges that are common there. Located just south of Shark Hotel, depths average sixty feet above the wall ... and 200 feet at the bottom of the wall. In addition to the numerous sponges, both macro- and wide-angle photographers will enjoy the large clusters of acorn coral scattered around the reef. Keep an eye out for large pelagics that often come in from deeper water to feed.

Perhaps the most spectacular sights on the wall are the gigantic elephant ear sponges, which often measure ten feet across.

Shark City: Although I didn't actually dive this site, locals insist that sharks are encountered on every dive. A sloping bottom from fifty to ninety feet, where the wall begins, is sandy and home to numerous stingrays. Reef sharks are said to cruise the deeper sections of the wall, where local guides tell me they have been feeding them on a semi-regular basis. Conditions in the area can be rough, making this a fair weather-only diving site.

Elkhorn Reef: Named after the large branches of elkhorn coral that almost break the surface, this site is ideal for both snorkelers and scuba divers. The bottom slopes gently down to fifty feet, where a short drop to one hundred feet will be encountered. Photographers and sightseers alike will enjoy the numerous corals, sponges, various species of fish, and spidercrabs commonly found in the area.

Since the early 1980s, Providenciales has been home to "JoJo" the Dolphin. JoJo regularly seeks out human contact and swims with bathers around the islands. Numerous magazine articles, TV shows, and documentary films have been made about this amazing animal, attracting tourists and dolphin watchers from around the world.

Elkhorn coral provides protection to a red hind.

26 | The Caicos Islands

A visit to Turk or Providenciales wouldn't be complete without a stop at the Caicos Islands. Generally referred to as East Caicos, Middle Caicos, North Caicos, and South Caicos, these islands offer some of the most spectacular unexplored reefs in the Caribbean.

Middle Caicos is the largest island of the group and takes up approximately forty-eight square miles. It has been long well-known to cave explorers and naturalists, who often visit the island to observe and photograph the numerous "bat caves" common on Middle Caicos. In fact, many of the caves were mined for bat droppings used for fertilizers during the 1880s.

East Caicos takes up twenty-six and one-half square miles and was first inhabited by Tainos Indians during the 1600s. Naturalists often visit the area to photograph and observe the numerous tame iguanas East Caicos is known for.

North Caicos, with a population of 1,300, takes up forty-four square miles and offers tourists numerous non-diving activities in addition to world-class diving. *Flamingo Pond*, in particular, is worth a visit. Photographers can photograph the thousands of flamingos that live here.

South Caicos is home to 1,200 inhabitants and is eight and one-half square miles in size. Long well-known to sailors who participate in the annual South Caicos Regatta, the island attracts visitors from all over the world.

Some of the most popular dive sights are:

Blue Hole: This large circular sinkhole is 400 yards in diameter and 200 feet deep. Visiting the area requires passage with a knowledgeable captain, since it's easy to run aground on the numerous sandbanks common to the area. Known for the large pelagics that can be found in the hole, this site should please photographers and sightseers alike.

Eagle Ray Reef: Located off South Caicos, Eagle Ray Reef is well-known for the numerous species of coral that can be found on its sloping bottom. Depths range from thirty-five to eighty feet, making this an ideal site for novice divers when the currents in the area aren't strong.

The Caicos Islands can provide you with many incredible diving experiences.

27 | Silver Banks

"I didn't know fish got that big," said Oliver in wide-eyed disbelief, as the humpback whale's tail slowly sank below the surface fifty feet in front of our launch.

"It's not a fish, Oliver, it's a mammal, and some species get almost twice as big!" I yelled over the noise of the throbbing engine.

Oliver's reaction was to begin to turn the boat away and head back towards our mother ship, *Coral Star*, anchored one and one-half miles off our stern. It took a few minutes of deliberation before he was convinced that the whale wouldn't behave like Moby Dick and smash our twenty-foot boat into a thousand splinters. The fact that we had witnessed dozens of whales breaching (jumping almost clear of the water) during the last few days wasn't helping matters!

We were at Silver Banks, located seventy-five miles off the coast of the Dominican Republic, almost directly off the city of Puerto Plata. The purpose of the trip was to photograph and observe the hundreds, if not thousands, of humpback whales that annually migrate to the area during the first three months of the year to breed and give birth. Silver Banks is the east coast equivalent (as far as the whales are concerned) to Kona in Hawaii. The west coast humpbacks migrate from Alaska to Hawaii, while the east coast humpbacks migrate from the northern Atlantic to Silver Banks. While numerous restrictions protect the whales off Hawaii (which is necessary since people can practically reach them by swimming from shore), no such restrictions have been set for the whales at Silver Banks, since reaching the area requires effort and knowledge.

The banks don't offer much to sightseers other than the whales, since the Dominican Republic has been fishing the banks for years and they are fairly depleted of large marine life. Depth in the area is a consistent eighty feet — except for the large pillars of coral that rise to within inches of the surface. Keep in mind if you plan to travel to this area by private boat that navigating these submerged coral heads is extremely tricky and dangerous at best. A 300-foot freighter that went aground in 1983 sits as a testimonial to the navigational hazards in the area.

An interesting group of children can be found living on this wreck, under the supervision of the Island Expedition organization. These youngsters live off the sea and learn about the marine environment while practicing "survival skills" by living on the wreck.

The most amazing thing about Silver Banks is, of course, the whales, which can be seen in one of three ways. First, you can observe them from an anchored mother ship. At any given moment, you will be able to observe at least two or three whales breaching, spy-hopping (raising their heads out of the water to look around), blowing, and slapping their flukes (tails) or flippers against the water. If you have a good telephoto lens, it is possible to take some spectacular photographs in this manner. In fact, we had whales surface within fifty feet of our boat on numerous occasions.

If you would like to observe the animals a little closer, you may want to use a fast inflatable boat such as a zodiac. The best method is to slowly approach an area where you see whales blowing (exhaling). Usually, they will sound (dive) as you draw near. At this point, idle the boat and wait. Chances are, the whales will surface after a few minutes ... often right next to your boat! On one such trip, we witnessed two male humpbacks "fighting" over a female. Oliver later told me he was extremely frightened of the whales overturning our launch. I didn't tell him ... but so was I.

If you want to get in the water with the whales, you can have the inflatable drop you off in front of their swim path ... at which point you will skin-dive down thirty or forty feet and hope the whales swim by! Scuba gear isn't needed since the bubbles seem to scare the animals away and you will have a hard time getting in and out of the boat quickly as the whales move.

A humpback whale surfaces at Silver Banks.

A wreck provides the only "landmark" at Silver Banks.

Nicolas Popov, founder of Island Expeditions, leads a group of children around the Caribbean. Three months are spent living on this wreck at Silver Banks, seventy-five miles off the Dominican Republic.

28 | The Cayman Islands

Located south of Cuba and west of Jamaica, the Cayman Islands are made up of Grand Cayman, which is the largest and most commercially developed of the group, and the two smaller islands of Little Cayman and Cayman Brac. While not as primitive as many other Caribbean destinations, Cayman offers what I believe to be the best all-around diving in the Caribbean.

An enjoyable (or unenjoyable, depending on your perspective) aspect of the Cayman Islands is the fact that they are extremely commercialized. Four star restaurants abound — but you can also go to the local Burger King. Most of the hotels are located along "Seven Mile Beach" and offer numerous activities such as windsurfing, parasailing, water-skiing, and, of course, diving. Cayman attracts almost as many non-diving tourists as it does divers.

Somebody once told me that there were more banks on the islands than hotels and restaurants combined. Long known as a tax-free financial haven, Cayman's banking industry attracts an international clientele.

The islands were first discovered in 1503 when Columbus was blown off course during his fourth voyage to the New World. He named the island Las Tortugas, after the turtles that are common to the area. In fact, turtle meat became a main source of food for sailors traveling in the Caribbean. When visiting Cayman, you may want to take some time to visit the turtle farm, where you can observe and handle some of the thousands of turtles that are raised there. It is, however, illegal to bring turtle shells back to the U.S.

Sir Francis Drake mentions the Cayman Islands in his log of 1586, as does Captain William King, who came ashore to collect fresh water in 1592.

Water temperature in the Caymans averages 80 degrees ... and 200-foot visibility isn't uncommon! Some of the "must-see" dives at Cayman are:

The *Balboa*: Located off Georgetown in thirty feet of water, this wreck has long been a favorite of photographers in Cayman. The propeller in particular makes a good subject for wide-angle compositions.

The wreck has become home to numerous species of marine life in an otherwise relatively barren environment. Look for lobster, moray eels, numerous squirrelfish, and large angelfish living in the wreck. Exploration of the sandy bottom will reveal numerous flatfish and an occasional stingray.

Most dive operators run night dives on this colorful wreck.

Schooling barracuda can often be approached by divers.

The *Oro Verde*: This 180-foot cargo ship was purposely sunk in 1980 to create a reef for visiting divers. Situated about one-quarter mile offshore in front of the Holiday Inn, the wreck is home to quite a few barracuda and is decorated with numerous macro-subjects that will delight closeup photographers. This is an excellent wreck for novice divers — depths are thirty to fifty feet, and currents are mild.

The Aquarium: As its name implies, this is an excellent site for fish photography/sightseeing. With depths in the thirty-foot range, novice divers will enjoy this reef. Relatively tame angelfish, parrotfish, blue indigo hamlets, eagle rays, groupers, and red hinds are all common.

Pinnacle Rock: A wall dive to remember! This is one of those sites where you look down and wonder if it ever ends. The chances of encountering big animals here are high, since they occasionally wander in from deeper water as they pass the island. As with many sites in the Cayman Islands, large barrel sponges are abundant. Although these sponges are large enough to swim inside, resist the temptation to do so since you may damage the animal.

You may want to invest in a computer before traveling to the Cayman Islands, since many of the dive guides get "nervous" about depth and time when diving the seemingly bottomless walls common off Cayman.

Bloody Bay Wall: Bloody Bay Wall is one of the premiere wall dives off the northeast side of Little Cayman. The wall begins in twenty feet of water and drops into the abyss. This is a great place for photography since visibility is almost always terrific and the large sponges, Gorgonians, turtles, and colorful fish all make terrific photographic subjects.

Turtles are commonly seen along this wall. If you should be lucky enough to encounter one, resist the temptation to "ride it." Turtles are reptiles and must return to the surface to breathe like whales and dolphins. By holding onto the animal you may tire it out and accidentally drown it. Or, you may use up the animal's strength, making it incapable of returning to the surface after you let it go.

29 | Stingray City

"Take your snorkel off your mask," the divemaster was explaining. We were about to make a dive at Stingray City off Grand Cayman Island. "The stingrays have learned that a snorkel is a lot like a slot machine handle. If they grab your snorkel and pull on it, your mask floods and you have to let go of the food you're holding to clear your mask. The stingrays know that the more snorkels they pull at, the bigger the pay-off!"

Samantha, a newly certified diver from New York, who had traveled to the Caymans to do research for a new script she was writing, was looking over the side with obvious apprehension. "Don't these things have some kind of stinger?" she asked.

"Yes," the divemaster replied. "Midway down their tails is a thick spike that points towards their body. They can't sting you with the ends of their tail as is commonly believed — but are capable of sticking you with the barb by lifting their tails over their heads and stabbing you."

Samantha didn't look pleased.

The divemaster continued: "Don't worry, however; we've been coming here for years and have never had an accident."

"Which means you'll be the first," Chipper smiled.

"Actually," the divemaster explained, "the stingrays have become quite accustomed to divers and seem to consciously keep their tails clear of our bodies. It's a simple case of not wanting to bite the hands that feed them. The animals are aware that the barb on their tail is used for defense when under attack … and they know we're not attacking."

Samantha didn't seem to be listening. She was busy looking at the two dozen stingrays that had gathered fifteen feet below our boat. The animals have learned that shortly after the boats arrive, food-carrying scuba divers enter the water.

"Let's go!" said an enthusiastic Chipper, as we all entered the water. As soon as we reached the bottom, stingray madness began. There were stingrays sucking on our hair, stingrays probing our B.C.s, stingrays between our legs, and stingrays pushing on our backs.

After a few moments, I became aware that my underwater flash was firing continuously … except I wasn't taking pictures. As I attempted to advance the film in my Nikonos, it jammed. "Great," I thought, "another flooded camera." Lately, I seemed to be destroying cameras at a rate of about one a month and it was getting expensive! Looking to the right, the misery over my non-functioning camera increased when I saw Samantha calmly feeding a large stingray while Chipper looked on.

One of the nice things about Stingray City is the shallow depth, which allows you unlimited bottom time. If you bring a camera (assuming you don't fill it with water), don't rush into picture taking, but spend a few minutes to absorb and enjoy the experience while the animals settle down. Remember, you will most likely have an hour of bottom time.

Christmas tree worms in the Caribbean.

30 | Santa Rosa Island

Located twenty-six and one-half miles off the coast of Ventura, California, Santa Rosa is the second largest of southern California's Channel Islands and offers divers high adventure at an affordable price. The island sits six miles off the west end of Santa Cruz, with San Miguel lying three miles off the east end. Along with Anacapa, these four islands are often referred to as southern California's "northern Channel Islands."

Santa Rosa's shoreline is primarily made up of jagged cliffs and sandy beaches. It is known for the large populations of abalone and lobster that can easily be found in the island's rocky bottom. Other areas are made of sandy spots where good-size halibut are often taken. The abundant game and relatively short boat ride from the mainland make Santa Rosa a favorite of game hunters.

There are four exciting known diveable wrecks off Santa Rosa. The *Aggi*, off the northwest end of the island, is the most frequented, and well-known to bug hunters. The *Crown of England*, in fifteen feet of water; the *Goldenhorn*, in twenty-five feet of water; and the *Dora Bluhm*, in fifty feet, are all diveable wrecks.

The 459-foot *Chichasaw* lies broken up above the water line just west of south point. While not a diveable wreck, it does offer some interesting above-water photo opportunities.

There is radiocarbon evidence that there may have been Indians living on Santa Rosa island as long as 10,000 years ago. When Spanish explorer Juan Rodriguez Cabrillo "discovered" the Channel Islands in 1542, he found Santa Rosa inhabited by Chumash Indians, who referred to the island as *Wima*.

Many people believe Cabrillo may be buried on Santa Rosa. In 1901, explorer Philip Jones found a thirteen-inch stone with a cross, and the initials J.R. carved on it. A few years ago, anthropologist Robert Heizer claimed this could have been Cabrillo's headstone.

In 1843, Santa Rosa was given to the Carrillo family. Two sisters eventually acquired sole ownership and moved to the island with their husbands to start a ranching operation. Santa Rosa is ideally suited to ranching, and by 1857 there were over 10,000 animals grazing on the island.

The More brothers took over ranching operations in 1858. They concentrated primarily on wool and increased the herd to over 100,000 sheep.

A garibaldi poses under the California sun.

One of the brothers, Alexander P. More, was known to be a hot-tempered man. When he caught his Chinese cook trying to sneak off the island, he shot him for desertion. In 1876, during a slow period in the wool trade, he slaughtered his sheep at a rate of 1,200 a day and sold the meat as pig food. Alexander More's son, John, took over managing the island after his father's death in 1893, but was fired from the position after he was caught embezzling $80,000 from the estate.

After continuing management problems, the island was sold to Vail & Vickers in 1902. Vail & Vickers removed all the sheep from the island and converted the ranching operation to accommodate cattle. In 1986, the United States government bought Santa Rosa from Vail & Vickers; the selling price was $29,850,250.

Beacon Reef off Carrington Point is a good spot for divers of all skill levels. The reef comes within twelve feet of the surface and slowly drops down ninety feet on the north side.

The sandy area between shore and the reef has produced some good-size halibut. Lobster hunters will do best along the deeper section of the reef. Visibility varies at this spot, with the average being about twenty feet. Photographers will find numerous macro-subjects in both the shallow and deeper areas of the reef. In calm weather, the top of the reef can be enjoyed by non-diving snorkelers.

East Point, at the easternmost end of the island, is one of Santa Rosa's best sites. Various reefs run south parallel to shore; the large kelp bed helps define the area.

Spearfishermen will find numerous game fish swimming through the kelp. Farther south, where the reef ends and the sandy bottom starts, is another good halibut spot.

Lobster can be found all over the reef. Abalone hunters will do best in the shallow areas. Some good-size scallops can still be found at various places along this reef.

The visibility at East Point is usually better than at some other sites around the island. Wide-angle photographers will find numerous photo opportunities in the kelp.

The U.S. Air Force once maintained a base at *Johnson's Lee*. Just south of what remains of an old pier is a sandy bottom. The reef from Ford Point approaches the northeast side of the pier, with depths in the fifteen- to eighty-foot range.

Wide-angle photographers should look for bat rays swimming through the kelp. Macro-photographers will find numerous subjects everywhere on the reef. Black sea bass have been reported at this site.

Lobster can be found in the shallows early in the season, and in the deeper areas late in the season. Ab hunters should do well in all areas. Johnson's Lee is one of the easiest dives on Santa Rosa.

Tom Maney examines a wreck off southern California.

South Point, just south of Johnson's Lee, is an excellent spot for ab hunters. The area is made up of rocky areas separated by large sandy patches.

Rockfish, sheepshead, cabezon, sculpin, and lingcod can be found on the reef; numerous angel sharks inhabit the sandy areas. Macro and midrange photographers will find subjects not found on some of the other Channel Islands. Large sun sea stars, unusual nudibranchs, and white sea cucumbers all make fascinating subjects.

Cluster Point, on the back side of the island, is occasionally visited by ab and/or lobster hunters. Water conditions can be rough — as a result, visibility is usually poor. The reef is about 200 yards offshore. Many areas on the back side of Santa Rosa are deceivingly shallow; private boaters should beware!

West of Cluster Point, about a mile offshore, lies *Bee Rock*. The sides of the rock drop down to about eighty feet. Spearfishermen like Bee Rock because of the occasional pelagic that swims by. White lined nudibranchs, sea lemons, yellow edged cadlinas, and numerous species of anemones will occupy photographers.

Off the northwest end of Santa Rosa is a twenty-square-mile area known as *Talcott Shoals*. This area is one of the best spots for game hunters in southern California. With depths ranging from twenty to one hundred feet, it offers something for everyone.

Like other spots around the island, lobster will be found in the shallows early in the season, and in deeper water late in the season.

Ab hunters usually do well at the shoals. The shallow areas are often overlooked, and usually prove productive.

White sea bass, perch, sculpins, rockfish, and numerous other species of fish can be found around the areas with kelp. Spearfishermen usually hunt the reef fish in the deeper areas where visibility is high. Visibility near shore is usually poor, but this is where halibut hunters will find the best results.

Photographers should visit the two wrecks in this area, if possible. The *Aggi* lies in sixty to eighty feet of water, and is covered with photogenic marine life. The *Golden Horn* lies in fifteen-foot water, and rough surge can make the area hazardous. Both wrecks are excellent sites for bug hunters.

31 | Cave Diving

Swimming in a cave, hundreds of feet beneath the water's surface, with hours of decompression ahead of you — assuming you can find your way back to the stage tanks that you left behind — is definitely one of the greatest adventures you can have underwater!

IT IS EXTREMELY IMPORTANT NOT TO ATTEMPT ANY KIND OF CAVE DIVING WITHOUT FIRST OBTAINING QUALITY INSTRUCTION FROM A CERTIFIED CAVE-DIVING INSTRUCTOR. Under no circumstances should you ever enter a cave on your own. Too many divers have died by carelessly entering into a cave, only to become disoriented … run out of air … and drown.

Cave diving can be divided into three categories:

Snorkeling: Actually, this would be more accurately defined as "cavern exploration." The Nohoch Nachich Cave, located eighty miles south of Cancun on the Yucatan Peninsula, features a cavern that is 600 feet wide and 30 feet high! The inside of the cavern is one hundred yards wide and home to a large population of bats.

It is possible to explore this cavern while snorkeling, since it's easy to keep the entrance in sight. Obviously, snorkelers should at no time venture around bends or turns that would disorient them by concealing the exit.

Cavern Scuba Diving: This should only be done with an instructor familiar with the cavern and qualified to guide you. Cavern scuba diving is done in the same area used by snorkelers, except it's done with scuba equipment. In other words, cavern divers also keep their entry/exit point in clear sight at all times. This activity can only be done in caverns, such as the Nohoch Nachich (which, incidentally, means the "big bird house"), that have a cavern large enough to make the activity safe.

Full Cave Diving: You must positively obtain instruction before engaging in this activity. Cave divers have laid 43,800 feet of #18 nylon line in Nohoch Nachich in Mexico. Penetrating hundreds of feet (or thousands) into a cave requires carrying "stage bottles." Stage bottles are scuba tanks that the divers carry (usually two but sometimes more) so that they don't use the air in the tanks strapped to their back. The usual procedure is to breathe one-third of the air in the stage bottles, at which point they attach the tank to their guideline, where it awaits their return on the way out. Obviously, it is extremely important that divers don't get disoriented during the dive, since returning to these tanks is imperative!

Redundancy is a way of life for cave divers. Imagine being 600 feet into a cave with lots of air … only to have your regulator fail. Not fun. Cave divers carry backup regulators, lights, tanks, and other redundant systems. Most of the divers exploring Nohoch Nachich wear double 104's on their back in addition to the stage tanks they carry. Another nice feature about the Nohoch Nachich cave system is that depths are shallow enough that decompression is not required. Some caves have a steep vertical drop, requiring divers to make long decompression stops on the way up.

Visibility in the Nohoch Nachich caves is unlimited, which is one of the things that draws cave divers into the sport. Naturalists travel to Nohoch Nachich to observe the Remepeeia, a small crustacean that was thought to be extinct until scientists recently "rediscovered" the one-inch, centipede-like creature. Photographers may want to keep an eye out for the numerous five-inch-long catfish that are also common in the area, as are the blind cavefish (*Lucifuga speleotes*). Water temperature in the caves is 78 degrees.

32 | Ice Diving

Ice diving combines the excitement and dangers of cave diving with the harshness of winter. Cutting a hole in a frozen lake with a chain saw and then jumping in definitely qualifies as underwater adventure!

As with cave diving, ICE DIVING REQUIRES THAT YOU FIRST OBTAIN QUALIFIED INSTRUCTION FROM A CERTIFIED ICE DIVING INSTRUCTOR. You definitely do not want to engage in this activity without supervision.

The first thing ice divers must do is select a location that is safe. Obviously, setting up camp on thin ice isn't desirable. Chain saws are used to cut an opening in the ice large enough for two or three divers to enter and exit from. Usually, a tent or some form of shelter is set up over the hole to provide protection from the elements. Safety lines are an important part of ice diving since a diver's survival depends on his ability to relocate the hole in the ice when it is time to get out. But what should you do if you become "unattached" from your safety line? The most important thing to remember is to *stay put*. Chances are you will only become increasingly disoriented if you try to conduct a search on your own. Obviously, surface personnel must be monitoring you the entire time you are in the water (through rope tugs, etc.), so they will be immediately aware if you have a problem. It is also important to have rescue divers standing by … geared up and ready to enter the water should there be a need.

One rescue/search technique commonly used by rescue divers is to swim in circles — while holding a rope — keeping the entry hole in the center. The idea is to increase the circle's diameter with each lap until they come across the diver in need. Should they miss the diver "visually," the rope (the other end of which is being held by surface personnel) will catch on the diver's body. Obviously, this assumes the diver who needs rescuing is not submerged, but waiting to be rescued just under the ice.

Redundancy is extremely important when ice diving. Backup systems are a must. It is also important that regulators don't freeze while submerged under two feet of ice!

The above information is not intended to replace qualified instruction. Before going ice diving, it is imperative that you obtain certified instruction. For example, I know of one incident when an ice diver's safety line was tied to a car's bumper that was parked onshore. The diver's problems really began when the owner of the car decided to go for coffee.

Incidentally, visibility under the ice is often "unlimited" — which is one reason ice diving can become so addicting. Standing upside down on the ice "ceiling" is also an experience most divers never forget.

33 | Matagi Island, Fiji

Carol Kurop is one of the nicest resort owners you will ever meet, which may account for the extremely high percentage of return customers to her operation on Matagi Island. Located east of Vanua Levu in the group of islands that make up Fiji, this 240-acre island is rapidly becoming one of the most sought-out destinations in the south Pacific. In fact, if you plan to visit the resort, you may want to make your reservations at least six months in advance.

So, what's so great about Matagi? Well, one of the nicest features is the fact that you will spend your visit onshore in the comfort of one of the ten individual *bures* (bungalows), which are decorated in traditional Fijian style and have queen-size beds along with an additional sofa bed. Each bure has a large private bathroom with modern facilities.

The dive center, located on the beach, is a short walk away and is ready to assist divers with instruction, rental equipment, and friendly service. *Friendly* is the word that keeps coming to mind when describing any aspect of this resort!

In addition to the onshore facilities, divers have the option of making two tank "day" dives on either the thirty-one-foot *Marama Ni Mataga* or the forty-two-foot *Lady Christene*, both of which carry a maximum of ten divers.

Or you may choose to spend part of your vacation on the resort's sixty-foot live-aboard vessel, the *Matagi Princess*. When it comes to exclusive comfort and style, the *Matagi Princess* is Number One! The ship only carries six guests (although they could pack in more, but don't) in spacious, air-conditioned cabins. With 15,000 gallons of fresh water on-board, divers are free to shower as often as they wish.

An ideal vacation is to divide your time between the live-aboard and the onshore facilities. Some of the excellent dive sites visited by the *Matagi Princess* include:

Moria's Cove: Located fairly close to Matagi, this is an excellent site for macro-photographers. Brightly colored nudibranchs, hawk fish, blennies, moray eels, goby, and other small subjects can be found everywhere. One of the most beautiful sights on these islands is the unique looking strands of red whip coral that can be seen at many sites.

Ringgold: Located fourteen miles north of Matagi, this is a series of about six uninhabited islands and barrier reefs. Some of the large coral heads in this area exceed ten feet in diameter! Other treasures include colorful crinoids that can be found attached to the large Gorgonians on the numerous wall dives around these islands.

Motualevu Reef: An excellent place for fish photography and sightseeing. Your chances of seeing sharks are excellent while diving this small atoll! Oceanic white tips may be seen cruising the deep water, while bronze whalers and other species are often encountered.

One of the highlights of Fiji is the large branches of soft coral that "bloom" when currents are strong. Divers often have to time their dives with tidal changes to ensure that the corals are out.

A goby apprehensively watches the photographer.

34 | San Nicholas Island & Begg Rock

"I guarantee 200-foot visibility along with more color than you've seen during any dive in California," Shelli was explaining, as the diveboat *Charisma* made its way towards San Nicholas Island. She was referring to Begg Rock, which is located eight miles off the west end of San Nicholas. Although the boat ride had been nearly eight hours, most people didn't seem to mind since we had been entertained by migrating gray whales along with a pod of killer whales.

San Nicholas Island is one of southern California's eight Channel Islands and is located farthest away from the mainland. While many divers are familiar with well-known Catalina, few seem to be aware of the large pelagic species of marine life, hundreds of sea lions, vibrantly colorful bottom terrain, and lush kelp beds typical of San Nicholas.

The island was first inhabited by Indians who were believed to have arrived "island hopping" out from the mainland in primitive canoes. Shortly after the Spanish arrived, they transported all the Indian inhabitants to the mainland ... or so they thought. In 1853, Captain George Nidever and Carl Dittmann visited San Nicholas and were shocked to find footprints! They followed the prints and found a lone woman. After offering food to her visitors, she gathered her few possessions and left the island quite willingly. Captain Nidever relocated her to Santa Barbara, where she was given the name Juana Maria. She explained that she had not left the island eighteen years ago when the other members of her tribe were relocated because her baby had been left behind. While she went back to the campsite to find her child, the ships left, leaving her in isolation for eighteen years! Sadly, she reported the child was killed by feral dogs, which ironically became her pets and only companions in later years. Since no one could understand her native tongue, Juana communicated through sign language and quickly became the town's most popular resident. Unfortunately, she died six weeks after her arrival, reportedly due to a weak immune system stemming from a lack of human contact.

The U.S. Navy currently has a missile tracking and guidance center on the island, where they train personnel for various duties, including tracking the space shuttle. Civilians are not allowed on San Nicholas unless they first obtain permission from the Navy, and there is a 300-yard buffer zone surrounding the island. Diveboats and personal recreational boats are not allowed to penetrate this perimeter.

Recently, forty-nine sea otters were relocated to San Nicholas Island. Amazingly, some swam back to the mainland ... surviving the seventy-mile crossing! At least one animal was found shot. The otters will occasionally approach divers, giving them a unique opportunity to observe these animals underwater.

The California Department of Fish & Game has a lobster-tagging program in operation around the island. If you capture a "bug" with a yellow marker, you should contact the Department or the University of Santa Cruz and tell them where you found the animal.

California purple hydrocoral can be seen at some of the Channel Islands.

Photographers may encounter the now rarely seen black sea bass at various sites around the island. Since the island is relatively far from the mainland, all marine life in the area is noticeably larger than at Catalina Island. Visibility averages one hundred feet, but I've seen 200 feet on quite a few occasions at Begg Rock. Colors underwater are equal to the vibrant colors usually only seen in the tropics. The large red rose anemone should delight the macro-photographer.

If you are anxious to get in the water with sea lions, this may be a dive for you! A large male can weigh in at close to 700 pounds and be ten feet long. Having one of these animals rush at you only to veer away two feet from your mask is a thrill all divers should experience.

The following areas offer some of the best diving around the island:

Seven-Fathom Reef: Three miles off the west end of San Nicholas, this reef offers one of the best wall dives in the Channel Islands. Macro-photographers will enjoy the numerous sea stars, urchins, nudibranchs, sea hares, tubeworms, and other colorful subjects. Wide-angle enthusiasts will benefit from the terrific visibility and abundant marine life.

Dutch Harbor: Located on the southeasterly coast of the Island and a good alternate site when other areas of the island are inaccessible due to foul weather. With some of the shallowest depths around San Nicholas, Dutch Harbor is also ideal for the novice diver.

Three-Mile Reef: Located off the northern shore, this is a fascinating site made up of canyons and deep drop-offs with depths averaging eighty to one hundred feet. Like Begg Rock, this is an open-water dive, best left to experienced divers. Spearfishermen enjoy the reef due to the abundance of large sheepshead, barracuda, opaleye, yellowtail, various species of bass, sculpin, and rockfish.

The Boilers: Located about two miles off the west end of San Nicholas, its name derives from the reef just below the surface that churns the water up, creating the illusion that the ocean is "boiling." Visibility in the area often isn't as good as at other sites around the island, but game hunters report fantastic results. Record-size lobster and large abalone are often taken here. Keep in mind that currents in the area can be treacherous.

Begg Rock: Located eight miles off the west end of San Nicholas, this is one of my personal favorite dive sites in the world! With visibility in the 200-foot range (on a good day), vibrant colors, large pelagics, and diverse marine life, this site offers something for everybody. Unfortunately, Begg Rock is a hit-or-miss situation weather-wise. While I have had some of the most memorable dives in calm seas ... I've also had boat rides out to the area that were so horrible I swore I would give up diving permanently.

35 | Truk Lagoon

Located in the Caroline Islands, Truk Lagoon offers unequaled wreck diving opportunities for the adventurous diver. Before our trip there, our guide had told us that we would be amazed at the size of some of the wrecks. "Yeah, sure," I thought. During my first dive on the *Shinkoku Maru*, I was truly amazed how long it took me to swim what I thought was the length of the ship. The real shock came when I reached the end ... only to look down and realize I had actually swum across the width of the boat. With a length of 504 feet, the *Shinkoku Maru* has to be seen to be believed!

There are approximately fifty Japanese shipwrecks and five aircraft wrecks in Truk Lagoon; mostly the result of a series of U.S. air raids that began on February 16, 1944.

The Japanese took control of the island from the Germans after the start of World War I in 1914. The lagoon and surrounding islands are a natural harbor with built-in defenses that by early 1900 standards were hard to penetrate. The forty-mile diameter lagoon, with a maximum depth of 300 feet, is protected by an outer coral reef that is almost 150 miles in circumference. In fact, American naval planners thought of the lagoon as practically impenetrable.

Overconfidence in the area's natural defenses may have contributed to the lack of preparedness by the Japanese. With a limited budget, the Japanese navy chose to channel their funds into the fleet rather than land-based facilities.

Operation HAILSTONE was conceived by Admiral Raymond A. Spruance and was originally set for April 15, 1944. Following the success of raids in the Marshall Islands, however, it was decided to move the attack forward to February.

Diving the wrecks of Truk Lagoon is an unforgettable experience and definitely cannot be done in one or two weeks. Some wrecks, such as the *Fujikawa Maru*, require several dives during the day along with at least one night dive! Some of the more famous wrecks in the lagoon are:

Fujikawa Maru: This is by far one of the most beautiful wrecks in Truk. With depths ranging from just a few feet below the surface (for the mast), to ninety feet (the deck), to below one hundred feet (the bottom), this wreck offers something for divers of all skill levels.

Built in 1938, the 434-foot-long *Fujikawa Maru* was one of ten merchant ships that were converted into aircraft transports when the war began. She was attacked by a U.S. submarine in 1943, but survived and continued service until she was sunk during the February 1944 raids.

Many of the wrecks in Truk can be seen with skin-diving equipment since they are close to the surface.

One of the most amazing sights is the nearly intact airplane in one of her cargo holds. If you are diving with a group, try to get into the ship's cargo holds (on any ship you're diving) ahead of other divers, who may stir up silt.

The *Fujikawa* may be the most photogenic wreck in the lagoon. The bow gun is covered with colorful sponges and other marine growths along with a small plaque put there by the manufacturer. Numerous large, soft coral branches decorate the entire hull of the ship.

Another nice aspect of this wreck is that it is safe (currently) to penetrate certain areas. The upper superstructure opens into a large room where rays of sunlight burn into the darkness, creating dramatic available light opportunities.

Shinkoku Maru: Built in 1940, the 504-foot *Shinkoku Maru* was built as a commercial tanker and was one of five oil tankers servicing the Japanese navy. Three things stand out about a dive on this wreck. First, the large gray reef sharks that can be seen cruising along the hull make for exciting viewing and photographs. Second, the wheelhouse still contains the control wheel, a lantern, a telephone, and other unique items. Third, the soft coral trees growing in the bow section of the hull are some of the most beautiful in the lagoon. Also, be sure to take time to examine the small bow gun, along with the numerous bottles, records, syringes, and, perhaps most interesting of all, the box of coins that your guide may show you inside the wreck.

The ship was probably sunk by the large hole that can be seen on her port side ... perhaps the result of a torpedo.

Nippo Maru: This 350-foot-long wreck is one of my personal favorites because of the Japanese tank that sits on its deck almost in the center of the ship. Also, at 160 feet, it is one of the deeper wrecks in the lagoon. Experienced divers (preferably with computers) will enjoy exploring the numerous war materials such as the two-foot-long artillery shells and antitank guns. One of the most interesting finds on the ship is the two bronze four-foot-long range finders that were used to determine the distance between the ship and attacking aircraft. A visit to the ship's wheelhouse will give you the opportunity to see the ship's telegraph and compass (which lies on the floor).

Heian Maru: The 500-foot-long *Heian Maru* was built in 1930 by the Nippon Yusen Kaisha at a cost of $15,000,000, with the intended purpose of supplying commercial passage between Japan and Seattle. Being state of the art for the era, she set a transpacific speed record on her maiden voyage in January 1931. At the outbreak of war, she was converted into a submarine tender by the Japanese navy.

Diving the *Heian Maru* requires you to acclimate yourself to the ship's sideways position (she rests on her port side). Depth ranges from forty feet

Some of the dive boats in Truk are fairly primitive.

(the ship's bridge) to below one hundred feet (sections of the bottom). Photographers may want to visit the bow, where the ship's name can still clearly be seen.

Other attractions are the two periscopes that can be found in one of the ship's passageways, along with the numerous gun barrels, personal artifacts, chains, cables, bottles, and plates that can be found scattered around the wreck. It seems to me that I've seen more plates, cups, and dishes on this wreck than any other.

Kensho Maru: The 384-foot *Kensho Maru* was found resting on a 130-foot bottom in 1980 by Klause Lindmann. Depths range from sixty feet (the superstructure) to the 130-foot bottom. Some of the better-known aspects of the wreck are the numerous ammunition boxes, the ship's compass, piles of china, radio equipment, numerous sake bottles, guns, and other war materials.

Gosei Maru: With a length of 272 feet and a width of forty feet, the *Gosei Maru* is not one of the larger ships in the lagoon. It is, however, a favorite of photographers, who are drawn to the large four-bladed propeller that lies thirty feet below the surface. Since the ship lies on her left side, some acclimation is required to ensure you see everything. The number two hold contains some torpedo shells and large crushed containers, all of which make for interesting photography.

36 | Kwajalein

Kwajalein, located in the Marshall Islands east of Truk and 2,400 miles southwest of Hawaii, is another location that offers world-class wreck diving adventures. The island is home to a U.S. missile range and supports over 2,000 army personnel. The island is one of thirty-three atolls and has a circumference of 180 miles.

First occupied by the Spanish during the nineteenth century, Kwajalein was later taken over by Germans, who occupied the island until 1914, when the Japanese captured them during World War I. Recognizing the area's strategic naval importance, the Japanese began to fortify the area.

Most of the ships in the lagoon were sunk during the U.S. raids that began on February 1, 1942 (two years prior to the raids on Truk). Considering the amount of effort required to travel to this part of the world, if you are visiting Truk you may want to spend a few dollars more to include Kwajalein in your itinerary. Some of the better known wrecks in the lagoon are:

Asakaze Maru: The 425-foot by 57-foot *Asakaze Maru* rests on a 160-foot bottom and is a favorite of photographers, who find the numerous brightly colored soft corals and sponges interesting subjects. There is a large gun on the bow that is covered with numerous corals and other marine growths. Other attractions include a car, piles of china, and an interesting maze of rigging suspended from the ship's superstructure.

Prinz Eugen: This 654-by-71-foot cruiser is one of the few non-Japanese ships in the lagoon. Named after Prince Eugene of Savoy, this German ship sits capsized, with its propellers above the water line. Photographers may wish to visit the torpedoes that can be found in the ship's interior. As with all wrecks that have potentially "live" explosives on-board, extreme caution should be exercised. I once watched a novice diver "land" on top of a mine following a negatively buoyant descent. Naturally, I had my camera poised in case he exploded!

Akibasan Maru: Believed to be the first wreck to be "discovered" in the lagoon, divers have been visiting this 375-foot wreck since 1965. The ship's deck sits in one hundred feet, where divers may encounter piles of china, numerous guns, coins, buttons, medals, sake bottles, navigational devices, and other items of war.

Seaplane pontoons can be found in the forward cargo hold, along with piles of brightly colored sake bottles. Be sure to check out the gun platform and unusual looking anchor winch while exploring the bow section.

Tateyama Maru: This 345-foot wreck lies on her starboard side on a 135-foot bottom and has probably been visited by more divers than any other wreck. It is known as the "bottle wreck" by local divers due to the seemingly endless array of glass bottles that can be found scattered around the bottom and in the ship's cargo holds. Photographers may want to visit the large smokestack that lies just off to the side.

What could be more adventurous than exploring a new wreck!

37 | U.S. Virgin Islands

Located just east of Puerto Rico, the U.S. Virgin Islands are part of the Antilles chain of islands. Visitors divide their time between the islands of St. Thomas, St. John, and St. Croix. If you are looking for a destination that offers excellent diving, but will also supply activities for your non-diving companions — the Virgin Islands may be for you!

St. John is the smallest island and known as the most secluded of the group. Due to the fact that the island is only nine miles long by five miles wide, St. John often appeals to divers who wish to get away from the crowds, but don't want to give up "Americanized" comforts.

Twenty-eight-mile-long St. Croix is the largest island in the group. Part of the island is very tropical in appearance with lush vegetation. Other areas, particularly the eastern end of the island, are much more arid — similar in appearance to the nearby British Virgin Islands.

St. Thomas is where the majority of the tourists go. This nine-mile-long island offers vacationers a full range of accommodations, restaurants, shops, and entertainment. You can have a charming tropical vacation — complete with beautiful beaches and crystal clear turquoise water — but still enjoy the modern comforts of civilization.

With water temperatures averaging 78 degrees and visibility generally exceeding one hundred feet, it's easy to see why so many divers make repeat trips to the Virgin Islands. Also, divers don't need to contend with the strong currents often found in places like Cozumel — making the Virgin Islands an ideal destination for novice divers. Some of the memorable dives in the Virgin Islands are:

Armando's Reef: Less than one-half mile from shore, Armando's Reef is one of the most frequently dove reefs off St. Thomas. Depth is in the twenty- to fifty-foot range, making this a good novice dive. The bottom is made up of flat areas and small drop-offs. Clusters of coral rise up a few feet from the bottom, and various species of fish can be found hiding in the protection of the coral's branches. A prized find for macro-photographers is the spiny oysters that are camouflaged with small sponges. Photographing one of these creatures in the "open" position is quite a challenge.

French Cap Cay: This lies south of St. John and requires an hour boat ride to get there. Massive growths of elkhorn coral supply impressive backdrops for diver pictures at most sites off the Cay. One of the dives you should definitely make (providing your skills match the conditions) is the *Pinnacle,* a seamount that begins in fifty feet of water and is one of the best locations for underwater photography in the Virgin Islands.

Katrina poses for a "dive" calendar in the U.S. Virgin Islands.

Fredericksted Pier: Off St. Croix, this is often dove at night due to its easy access. Keep an eye out for the unusual looking batfish that are occasionally seen. Macro-photographers will find an endless variety of subjects growing on the pier's pilings. It also is an enjoyable dive during the day, with the pilings supplying unique photo opportunities.

38 | Lobster Diving in California

Every October, hundreds of California divers anxiously await the first Wednesday of the month. In fact, some of them can be seen posed in their dive gear along the beach at 11:59 P.M. so that they can be the first to enter the water at the stroke of midnight — a sure sign of "bug fever."

Hunting lobster is an adventure that any certified scuba diver can partake in. Ideally it should be done at night, so some training in night diving procedures should be obtained first. How do you catch a lobster?

The best method is to go diving after dark in an area that has lots of rocky crevices on the bottom. The "bugs" hide in these areas in the day, and then come out at night to feed. You may be able to locate lobsters during the day by looking for their antennae sticking out from under a ledge, but catching the bugs while they are lodged in a crevice is difficult. The usual procedure (during the day) is to grab their antennae and slowly walk your hand up their antennae until you get a firm grip on their body.

A much easier method is to go diving at night when the lobsters are feeding and can be found walking along the bottom in the open. When you see a lobster, shine your light directly in front of him ... this momentarily causes him to freeze in his tracks. I suppose it would be similar to walking down a dark street and suddenly have the sun instantly appear!

Take advantage of the lobster's stunned state of mind and grab him quickly with your other hand. It's important to aim for the bug's body and to push down to "pin" him to the bottom. A lobster's tail is capable of cutting your hand when it flexes (which is how it swims). For this reason, you don't want to grab the tail ... and you want to wear protective gloves. With smaller lobsters it is possible to overpower the animal's tail.

If you are diving with a buddy, he can shine the light in the lobster's face while you approach and grab from the rear. This method has the added advantage of allowing you to block the animal's escape with your body in the unlikely event it "bolts" when the lights go on!

So now you're sitting on the bottom of the ocean with the lobster in one hand and wondering where to put it. The most common method is to carry a "game bag" hooked to your belt. Since lobsters swim backwards, it is important to place them in the bag backwards. Most divers get smacked in the face by the fleeing lobster as it "rockets" out of the bag as soon as they release their hold on it. Placing the bug in backwards helps prevent this. Another method is to have your buddy hold the animal's body from outside the bag as you remove your hand from the bag.

California lobsters don't have claws like the ones in New England. If you go lobster hunting in an area where the animals have painful pinchers, extra caution should be practiced! Be sure to know local fish and game regulations in addition to obtaining a current fishing license.

A lobster hunter's dream come true!

39 | Shark Frenzy

"Today's dive ... is a shark dive," the divemaster was explaining.

"What?" said a suddenly apprehensive-looking Christine. Considering the fact that this was only her third dive since becoming a certified diver, her concern was understandable.

"Don't worry," we explained. "These are blacktip reef sharks that have absolutely no interest in divers. That is what's so nice about these reefs in Palau — the sharks are friendly."

Well, perhaps "friendly" was not exactly an accurate adjective ... but we all wanted to calm Christine down so that we could get on with the dive.

"Want to dive with me?" asked Tom.

"Sure," said Christine. "But let's not get too close to the sharks."

As the two of them descended to sixty feet where the wall began, Christine began to feel calm and confident. Surrounded by gigantic Gorgonians, colorful reef fish, and massive circular corals, Christine momentarily forgot about the sharks ... which didn't seem to be around anyway.

Twenty minutes later, Tom and Christine began their ascent from one hundred feet. Suddenly Christine felt a presence above her head and looked up.

"Oh my God," she thought as her heart suddenly seemed to be pounding audibly in her chest. "There must be twenty sharks up there."

Tom immediately recognized what was causing all the excitement. Six of the sharks were feeding on a large fish and were rapidly tearing it to shreds. Unfortunately, since Christine was now sucking down air at three times her normal consumption rate, the only solution was to ascend through the frenzied sharks to the safety of the boat.

"Let's go up," Tom signaled with the thumbs up signal used by divers when they want to ascend.

"Mmm ... Mmm ... Mmm," said Christine as she violently shook her head back and forth. Ascending definitely seemed like a bad idea as far as she was concerned. If anything, staying put seemed like a much better idea than swimming up through a bunch of hungry sharks!

"It's okay," signaled Tom. "Let's ascend." Actually Tom realized that Christine was becoming low on air, and he wanted to avoid an emergency situation ... such as a panicked, out-of-air bolt to the surface through a school of frenzied feeding sharks.

Shark diving is definitely an adventure.

The two of them slowly began their ascent while Tom held his tank in front of him to fend off any aggressive behavior. He later told me how amazed he was when he looked over at Christine and saw that the novice diver had removed her tank and was holding it assertively in front of her, ready to take on all comers! The fact that Christine was wearing a yellow tank and we had all told her stories about how sharks love "yum yum yellow" wasn't helping her state of mind.

Once back on the boat, the couple found out that one of the guides had speared some fish during the dive to attract sharks for the photographers in our group. Fortunately, we convinced Christine that not all dives in Palau involve ascending through shark-infested waters. When asked how she felt about the experience, the novice shark diver replied, "I felt lucky to be witnessing the event ... but I was also scared."

40 | Malibu Beach

The only time I have unexpectedly seen a whale underwater was off Malibu beach; that's reason enough for this stretch of southern California to rate high on my list of underwater adventures! Besides, ask a stranger to name the most famous beach in the world and the answer will probably be "Malibu"! What follows is a list of what I consider to be the best dive sites in Malibu.

Old Malibu Road is located about a mile past the Malibu pier. Turn to seaward off Pacific Coast Highway onto Web Way and then turn right onto Old Malibu Road. Beach access can be obtained through one of the vacant lots between the private homes. Another option is to launch a boat from Paradise Cove and motor down.

The sites off Old Malibu Road are the best Malibu has to offer. The reef is about fifty yards offshore and is marked by matted kelp on the surface. Game on these reefs is abundant, perhaps because of the limited access. Commercial lobster fishermen have been raiding this stretch of beach during the season for years. As far as "bugs" go, this is the place. Large nests of ten to twenty individuals are not uncommon finds.

Visibility along this beach can be as high as forty feet during the winter. The cleansing current that runs through the area keeps the water generally clearer than at other Malibu sites.

Photographers will find an endless variety of invertebrates. The reef is littered with sea stars, cowries, urchins, nudibranchs, sea hares, limpets, and tubeworms. A night dive off Old Malibu Road will also reveal a variety of photographic subjects. The only time I've seen a guitarfish was off this beach.

Malibu Reef is located in about sixty feet of water about one-half mile off the southern end of Old Malibu Road. It is only accessible by boat due to the long swim and heavy boat traffic. The reef was created in 1960 and is made of a few automobiles, a streetcar, some concrete blocks, and over 325 tons of rock.

Coral Beach is probably Malibu's most frequently dived site. Located just past Pepperdine University, Coral is the first public beach you will hit as you continue up Pacific Coast Highway past the school.

Coral Beach is another site used by local stores for checkout dives. The best place to make your entry is at the west end of the beach (Malibu's beaches face south). One reason for this is the walk to the water is easier at the west end of Coral.

The reef begins about twenty-five yards offshore and is marked by matted kelp lying on the surface. Visibility on a good day can be thirty feet, but five to fifteen is more common. Depth is in the twenty-five-foot range.

The best procedure is to swim out to where you see the kelp and start your dive once you have arrived. The reef basically runs parallel to the shore and is separated in spots by open sandy areas. Once you arrive at the kelp bed, check to see if there is a current running and start your dive into the current.

Coral is a good site for halibut and lobster hunters. Divers often come face to face with surprisingly large bugs when navigating through the eel grass. Results may be better in the shallows close to shore. Large sheep crabs are also frequently seen. Halibut hunters will do well in the outer sandy areas. Because so many classes use this site for checkout dives, keep an eye open for lost dive gear. Lost weight belts and knives are common finds at Coral.

The only public facilities at Coral are two portable outhouses. Parking is free along Pacific Coast Highway.

Escondido Beach is located just north of Coral at about 27144 Pacific Coast Highway. Parking is along the highway and access to the beach is by

A chestnut cowrie covers its shell with a mantle to keep it clean.

a short staircase. Lobster hunters visit Escondido during the season. The best results are said to be in the large patches of eel grass near shore.

Paradise Cove is located a little farther up Pacific Coast Highway from Escondido Beach. The address is 28128 West Pacific Coast Highway, but look for the large Paradise Cove turnoff sign.

Paradise Cove features a pier, a restaurant, boat launching facilities, and parking near the water. If you own a portable diveboat, you can launch it from Paradise Cove. In summer 1992, parking fees were about $8. Current cost information can be obtained by calling (213) 457-2511.

Visibility at Paradise Cove is generally poor. Depths are shallow, in the fifteen-foot range. Shell collectors will do well here. I've seen more cowrie shells while diving at Paradise than any other beach site. Kellet, mitre, and whelk shells are also common. It's a good policy to take only empty shells when collecting.

If you travel to the beach with non-diving friends or family members, Paradise Cove is a good place to go. Your expedition partners can watch you dive from the comfort of the beachside restaurant.

Point Dume is only accessible by walking south from Westward Beach, or by making the long two-mile walk from Paradise Cove. I recommend you only dive this area if you have a boat.

The Point Dume site is for experts only. At the buoy marker one-fourth mile out, depth is in the 500-foot range. The fact that it is that deep so close to shore means the chances of seeing a big pelagic fish are pretty high. That fact makes this area an all-time favorite with spearfishermen.

Westward Beach is located just south of Zuma. Turn off on Westward Beach Road and continue all the way to the end. There is a parking fee during certain times of year. The best diving is at the southeast end of the beach. Westward is an advanced dive. Beware of tricky currents and steep drop-offs.

The only time I've unexpectedly seen a whale while diving was at Westward Beach. Unexpected encounters with big animals are common at this site due to the deep canyon just offshore. Photographers be ready!

The bottom terrain is sandy with patches of reef. Depth increases quickly, so watch your depth. The drop-off at Westward is pretty steep; plan on depths in the sixty- to one hundred-foot range.

Visibility is generally better at this site than for most beach dives. Clear water from the deep canyon offshore cleanses the site year-round. Westward is a great site for photographers. In addition to large pelagic fish, octopi are also common finds. In fact, I've never *not* seen an octopus while diving Westward.

Zuma Beach, just northwest of Westward, is more famous for its surf than diving. However, when conditions permit, the area directly in front of the lifeguard facility is worth visiting.

A large bed of sand dollars will be encountered in about thirty feet of water forty yards offshore. Keep swimming and you will hit the largest pismo clam bed in southern California. There are also remnants left from a man-made reef just past the sand dollar bed.

It's a good idea to call ahead and get a surf report before making the drive to Zuma. On a few occasions, I've seen shore breakers over ten feet high at this site!

Encinal Bluffs is only accessible by walking/hiking down a three-fourth mile hill, or by boat. Located north of Zuma, these reefs are a favorite of hunters. This area has been left largely unexplored by divers because of its difficult access. Reports of great visibility and large game are the rule.

Leo Carrillo is about a ten-minute drive past Zuma and is Malibu's northernmost site. If traveling north on Pacific Coast Highway, turn right (away from the beach) into the campground area. There is a parking fee. Once past the ranger station, continue along the road until you get to the beachfront parking lot.

Visibility at Leo Carrillo varies, with ten feet being about the average. As with most of Malibu's sites, visibility is often poorer during the summer months.

Many lobster hunters and night divers call Leo Carrillo home. Depths are in the thirty-foot range around the kelp bed, which is located a short swim from shore.

Hunters frequent this site due to the variety of game fish that can be found swimming through the kelp. I've seen small schools of barracuda on a few occasions. Halibut and other flat fish may be encountered in the sandy areas that separate the reef.

41 | The Galapagos Islands

"The archipelagos is a little world within itself," is how Charles Darwin described the Galapagos Islands during his voyage on the English survey vessel H.M.S. *Beagle* in 1835. Darwin's book, *The Origin of Species*, which was inspired by his visit, brought worldwide attention to the islands.

Located 600 miles off the coast of Ecuador in South America, these islands have long enticed naturalists from around the world. The fact that the Galapagos Islands are so isolated contributes to them being such a wonderful living science field laboratory. Many species of plants and animals are indigenous to the islands.

Fray Tomas de Berlanga, who was the bishop of Panama, is credited with discovering the Galapagos Islands in 1535. Due to the barren landscape, no one settled on the islands, although whalers often stopped to collect meat of the giant tortoise (*Geochelone elephantopus*), whose numbers were greatly reduced by hunting.

Currently there are fewer than 12,000 people living on the islands. Almost ninety percent of the island is a national park that was established in 1959.

Trimarine's boat *Lammer Law* recently relocated to the Galapagos. Although I have not personally been on *Lammer Law*, I did spend an extremely enjoyable trip on the *Cuan Law*, which is almost identical in size and features (see Dive Adventure #5).

Duncan Muirhead tells me the divers have been having close encounters with marine iguanas, sea horses, dolphins, eagle rays, whales, octopi, the unique-looking slipper lobster, and the incredible-looking red-lipped batfish. Encounters with sea lions, seals, and other pinnipeds are unavoidable due to the over 50,000 individuals living there.

One of the aspects that makes the Galapagos so appealing is that you don't need to be a diver to witness the island's beauty. Bird watchers often visit the islands to observe the numerous endemic species, such as the waved albatross (*Diomedea irrorata*), Galapagos penguin (*Spheniscus mendiculus*), flightless cormorant (*Nannopterum harrisi*), Galapagos dove (*Nesopelia galapagoensis*), swallow-tailed gulls (*Creagrus furcatus*), and the Galapagos mocking bird (*Nesomimus parvules*).

Pufferfish are slow swimmers and make cooperative underwater subjects.

42 | Jamaica

Located south of Cuba and west of the Dominican Republic, 146-mile-long Jamaica is one of the largest islands in the Caribbean. Underwater terrain consists of wall diving for the most part, but there are also some shallow areas that offer excellent snorkeling. *Montego Bay* is the center of most tourist action. In fact, it's probably safe to say that every hotel has a dive operation, which is convenient considering that all dive sites are only a short boat ride away.

Runaway Bay is located about seventy miles from Montego Bay and is named after the Spanish, whom the British forced to flee the island. Divers will enjoy the recently sunk ship that is rapidly becoming an artificial reef. There's also an excellent wall dive said to have some of the most spectacular examples of black coral off Jamaica. Divers not wishing to make a wall dive may wish to explore the Cessna airplane that was sunk nearby.

Negril, to the west of Montego Bay, is another city often visited by divers. The one complaint some people have about Negril is that there is not much else to do except dive. *Blue Grotto* is an excellent dive off Negril and is made up of deep canyons inhabited by large schools of fish.

One thing to keep in mind about diving in Jamaica is their regulation that all diving *must* be done under the supervision of a divemaster. Depending on the divemaster, this can be a nice thing — or a royal pain.

Christmas tree worms can be found in most oceans of the world.

43 | Near Miss #1

Jon Hardy had been spearfishing for over an hour while the camp's cook, Frances, rowed the boat and supplied surface support. As a result of watching *Sea Hunt* each week, spearfishing had become a popular pastime during the 1960s.

The goal was to spear a shark to supply food for the camp. The year was 1964 and many of the camps around Catalina had to rely on food captured offshore.

Jon was skin diving since a scuba unit's exhaust bubbles tend to frighten fish away. A skin-diver can silently stalk his prey and move much faster through the water without the cumbersome drag of a tank, regulator, B.C., and heavy weight belt.

Luck seemed to be with the young Mr. Hardy on this day. Just as he was about to call it quits, Jon spotted a large leopard shark darting between the kelp along the bottom. Taking careful aim in front of the shark's swim path, Jon waited for the precise moment to fire his gun. Pop! The shaft propelled by three stretched pieces of rubber sailed through the water and struck the animal.

Before Jon could begin to reel the animal in, it bolted away and began swimming in circles, wrapping the spear's line around Jon's legs and the surrounding kelp.

"Oh my God," thought Jon, as he realized the line would prevent his return to the surface unless he took immediate action.

Swimming suddenly became impossible as the panicked fish continued to try to escape. With only two feet of water left between the surface — where life-preserving air awaited — Jon suddenly realized his entangled feet were preventing him from continuing his ascent.

"I'm going to die," flashed through his mind as he began to see stars, realizing unconsciousness was only seconds away.

From seemingly nowhere, two massive hands appeared and grabbed him under the arms. The amazing thing was that Frances not only lifted Jon clear of the water, but in her panicked state (realizing her companion was about to die), Frances lifted with such force that the shark, several feet of kelp, Jon, and his gun were all torn from the ocean only to land in a pile on the bottom of the boat.

The moral of the story is — don't skin-dive alone. If it hadn't been for the "surface support" of Frances, Mr. Hardy would surely have died.

Jon Hardy, owner of Argo Diving.

44 | Night Diving

Not all underwater adventures require extensive travel or great expense. With night diving it's possible to experience adventure — often "high adventure" — in your own backyard. Many creatures can only be seen at night. Basket stars, for example, stay curled in a tight ball during the day, but extend their arms at night to feed. Lobsters also "come out" at night. Many divers have observed moray eels from under a rock or reef during the day ... but imagine unexpectedly encountering one of these animals swimming freely at night! Once, during a night dive off Captain Don's habitat in Bonaire (an operation I highly recommend), I became aware of a "presence" behind me. As I turned to look over my left shoulder, a three-foot tarpon slowly slid along my cheek and flooded my mask! After the dive, it became apparent the fish had "dogged" other divers who were excitedly reenacting their encounter.

If you have never done a night dive, you should first obtain some instruction. Two things you must consider are: being able to see underwater, and being able to see your entry/exit point. Looking back at the shore from open water can be extremely disorienting since it is almost impossible to distinguish landmarks that are obvious during the day. Some divers leave a flashlight with a friend onshore, who continuously shines it out to sea. Another option is to have someone turn on his car's headlights after a predetermined amount of time. I've also found that Chem-lights™ left onshore make excellent markers. Since they come in different colors, you may want to leave one green and one red to mark your entry/exit "corridor."

Boats should also be well-lit during night dives. Few things will unnerve a novice diver faster than the feeling of being "lost" in the middle of the night ... in the middle of the ocean.

Obviously, you must also carry a light with you to see. My personal favorite is the Darrel Allan Bug Diver™, which is powered by ten D-cell batteries and bright enough to light up any environment. How bright a light you need has a lot to do with the conditions you are diving in. A night dive in Cozumel, for example, will probably take place in 78-degree water and one-hundred-foot plus visibility. In fact, you may be able to see the boat's lights while submerged! Conversely, a night dive on the wreck of the *Valiant*, off Catalina Island, may take place in thirty-foot visibility and 58-degree water. Having a powerful underwater light becomes an important safety factor.

It is a good idea to carry a secondary backup light in case your primary light fails. Having a second light will enable you to continue your dive versus having to make an ascent in total darkness … unable to read your gauges. Speaking of gauges, some glow in the dark and some don't. If you plan on doing a lot of night diving, you may want to look into this feature before you buy. Also, some computers have lights that illuminate them, obviously a useful feature for night divers.

Keep in mind that shining your light in your buddy's face, which is what most novice divers do when they want to explain something, blinds him. If you want to communicate something, hold your light at waist level and shine it on your face to illuminate what you are doing. Waving a light back and forth rapidly is a distress signal, so try not to do this unless you are in need of assistance.

Some divers attach chemical lights to their snorkels or tank valves so that they can be seen while on the surface. Divemasters will often hand out lights for this purpose. Attaching a chemical light to your tank valve helps your buddy locate you underwater when you have your back to him. It's amazing how you "disappear" when your body blocks your dive light. The glow of the chemical light helps your buddy locate you quickly in an emergency.

It's a good idea to first explore an area during the day before diving it at night. Some divers will make a late afternoon dive, go have dinner, and then come back and do a night dive. You don't want to discover nasty entanglements for the first time just as your dive light blacks out on your first night dive.

Wherever you do your first night dive, chances are it will be memorable. Few divers ever forget the adrenaline rush they experience the first time they descend into total blackness in the middle of some ocean or lake!

45 | The Coral Sea

Off the northern coast of Australia lies some of the clearest water in the world! If you are looking for adventuresome diving and relatively uncharted dive sites, check out the Coral Sea. While I haven't been there myself, a group of divers who recently returned told me about an "amazing" (their word, not mine) cluster of reefs located 130 miles northeast of Townsville. Known as *Flinders Reef*, this area can only be visited by boat ... and only by captains who have the experience and knowledge to avoid smashing into one of the coral pillars that rise up from the depths to within a few feet of the surface.

Stories of huge sharks and other animals are brought back by divers who have been there. Personally, I can't wait to go!

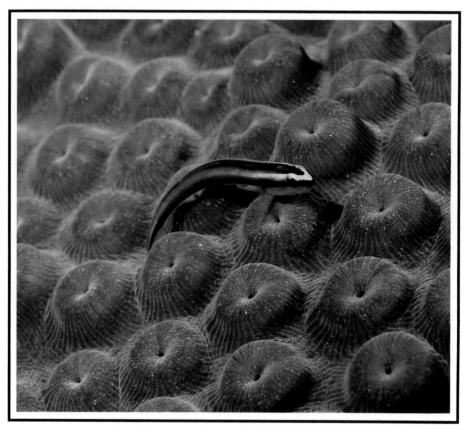

Sometimes looking "small" when diving will reveal colorful, never-before-noticed animals.

46 Heron Island

Located fifty miles off the coast of Australia, practically in the middle of the Great Barrier Reef, Heron Island is an ideal destination for divers since a seemingly endless number of dive sites can be visited along the barrier reef. The one drawback for some people is the fact that this is cold water (65 degrees, which I suppose isn't cold if you live in Minnesota in the middle of winter). If you desire true "tropical" diving, then Heron Island may not be for you!

Bird watchers often visit the island to photograph and observe the nearly 50,000 seabirds that nest there. Considering that the island is less than one-third mile long (and only 330 yards wide), it's understandable that there is only one hotel on the island ... plus a lot of birds.

Although I haven't been there (yet), this is another location high on my list of places I want to go. If you are looking for pristine diving, then Heron Island may be for you.

Macro subjects can be just as interesting as large animals.

47 | Near Miss #2

In the early 1960s, Jon Hardy and his companions collected various species of sharks for the aquariums at Marineland and Catalina. Having not yet developed the sophisticated techniques used today, they simply tied a rope around the shark's tail and then pulled it to the surface! A risky proposition at best.

Usually, the animals could be gently brought to the surface without incident. On one occasion, however, an angel shark (usually a docile species) almost cost Mr. Hardy his life.

The incident began in one hundred feet of water where Jon found a five-foot angel shark peacefully sleeping in the sand. Gently he placed the loop around the animal's body and then began to swim the rope to the surface where his crew waited on their twenty-foot boat. Once they knew a shark had been secured, they would begin gently pulling the animal in.

"This all took place in the middle of summer and so the water temperature wasn't too cold," Jon explained. "Back then I used to wear only my wet suit jacket during the summer. Suddenly, with the shark ten feet below the boat, there was a tremendous crash as the animal decided it didn't want to exit the water. Almost instantly I felt pain in the vicinity of my left thigh ... where the shark had bitten down and was now viciously chewing. Pandemonium began breaking out on the boat as they realized I had a five-foot shark attached to my leg, which definitely didn't appreciate being towed by the tail, and had decided to let me know how he felt in no uncertain terms.

"Remembering something I had seen on *Sea Hunt* about grabbing an animal by its gills to force it to let go — I did just that — placing my hand around the animal's mouth and gills. The moment it relaxed its jaws ... I let go. The moment I let go, however, the shark immediately bit down once again ... except this time it pinned my hand to my leg. In addition to the pain, the added problem of not being able to breathe suddenly became an immediate concern. Having been on the surface when the excitement begun, my regulator wasn't in my mouth. I was now rapidly sinking, unable to breathe, and had my hand and thigh inside the shark's mouth."

Jon was on the verge of blacking out when it suddenly occurred to him that if he let go ... then the shark might let go. With his last ounce of strength he reached out with his free hand and pulled the slipknot off the animal's tail. Instantly the fish turned and fled towards the bottom. "Looking back with the knowledge we have now, it's hard to believe we used such unsophisticated methods," Jon explained.

The damage to Jon's leg wasn't fully realized until he went to the doctor that night and was informed the shark had left exactly sixty-four small holes in his leg ... not to mention numerous lacerations on his hand and forearm.

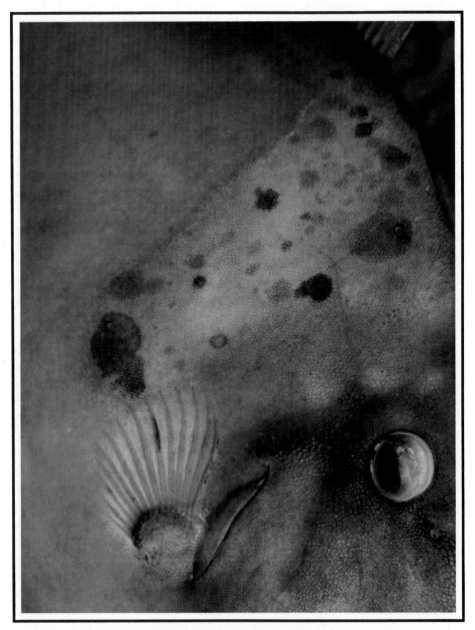

Filefish are common off many islands.

48 | Hawaii

Hawaii gives vacationing divers the chance to enjoy a wide variety of underwater adventures, beautiful tropical beaches, and world-class resort hotels ... all without leaving the United States. The fact that Hawaii is so isolated (about 2,000 miles from the nearest major land mass) adds to its mystique and tropical appeal.

Hawaii is the largest island in the Hawaiian chain and is usually referred to as "the big island." In addition to diving, there are numerous activities on the big island such as golf, horseback riding, hunting, mountain biking, motorcycle riding, just to name a few. Divers are attracted to the big island because of the tremendous variety in underwater terrain, which is a result of the island's size. Divers may encounter *manta rays* in open water, but can also dive sites close to shore that are inhabited by an endless variety of reef fish, including over ten species of butterflyfish.

Oahu is where the majority of the tourists visiting Hawaii go. Home to Pearl Harbor, the island is the most developed in the Hawaiian chain. Waikiki, in Honolulu, is a cluster of hotels, shops, restaurants, theaters, clubs, discotheques, and much more! Oahu is also relatively inexpensive. If you are looking for a dive trip, but are on a limited budget, you will probably find some appealing packages in Oahu. Two of the most popular dive sites off Oahu are:

Rainbow Reef: A nice site for novice divers since it's hard to get much deeper than thirty feet and currents are usually nonexistent. Don't be fooled, however, by the area's "student-like" status. There's a lot to see at Rainbow Reef. Fish photographers in particular will enjoy the reef, which is inhabited by colorful moray eels, pufferfish, filefish, kupipi, and an occasional scorpionfish.

Hanauma Bay: One of the most popular beaches, and one of the most beautiful, on Oahu. Snorkelers will enjoy the area's easy access and colorful underwater terrain. Numerous species of coral can be seen; this is an excellent place to bring people to introduce them to the underwater environment. The outer reef in sixty feet will appeal to divers. Keep an eye out for spotted eagle rays, which may be seen swimming along the outer edges of the reef.

The island of *Kauai* is more laid back and less developed than Oahu. One of the most popular dive sites is *Ahukini* on the windward side of the island. Since it is on the exposed side of the island, this area isn't always diveable; but when conditions are right, it's one of the best in Hawaii.

Some resorts offer vacationers a wide variety of watersports in addition to diving.

Maui, although not as developed as Oahu, is another island that is popular with vacationers. While the island has a "laid back" reputation, it's rapidly becoming a fast-paced resort. Windsurfing, in addition to diving, has become one of the islands primary water activities. Besides diving sites off Maui, excellent diving can be found off nearby *Lanai*.

49 | Santa Cruz Island

Located nineteen miles off the mainland, Santa Cruz Island is the biggest of southern California's Channel Islands. The ninety-six-square-mile island is twenty-two miles long and between two and six miles wide (about four times as big as Manhattan) and gives divers a chance to experience cold water adventure at an affordable price!

Because it is large, Santa Cruz offers a wide variety of diving environments. Water temperature can vary several degrees from one end of the island to another, and each temperature zone attracts a slightly different type of marine life.

Santa Cruz's underwater terrain includes shallow reefs that extend far offshore, while other areas are made up of sharp drop-offs and deep canyons. The variety in terrain and marine life is one reason many hunters favor the island.

Santa Cruz is also frequented by cave diving enthusiasts. Painted Cave, on the northwest end of the island, is the biggest sea cave in California. Many smaller caves can also be found around the island. Obviously, caves should be entered only by divers who are properly equipped and have obtained the proper training.

Photographers and wreck divers often travel to Santa Cruz to visit one of the most picturesque wrecks in the Channel Islands. Known as the "minesweeper," the 140-foot-long wreck is well worth a visit.

In 1769, the supply ship *San Antonio* arrived at Santa Cruz. Several of the crew, including a priest named Fray Juan Vizcaino, went ashore to meet the Indians. When they returned, Fray Vizcaino discovered that he had inadvertently left his walking staff onshore. Because the top of it was adorned with an iron cross, which would be valued by the Indians, it was given up as lost. As the ship prepared to leave, some of the crew noticed a group of Indians paddling out to the ship to return the lost staff. Fray Vizcaino was so taken by this act of kindness that he renamed the island "La Isle De Santa Cruz," meaning, "the island of the holy cross."

Scorpion Anchorage, on the north side of the island, is one of the most popular dive sites on Santa Cruz. Visibility is generally consistent because the anchorage is protected from most weather conditions.

Macro-photographers will do well at Scorpion, with numerous nudibranchs, feather-duster worms, urchins, sea stars, colorful anemones, and Gorgonians as common subjects. Lobster hunters will find the caves close to the shore filled with lobsters. Don't enter the caves, however, without adequate equipment and training.

Divers take a break for lunch between dives at Santa Cruz Island.

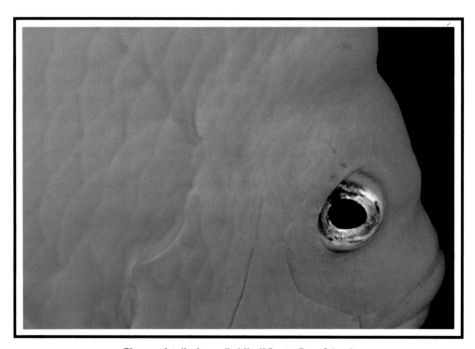

Closeup detail of a garibaldi off Santa Cruz Island.

The wreck of the minesweeper lies in sixty feet of water. This World War II ship went down in the early 1970s and is covered with colorful invertebrates, which makes it a favorite of photographers.

San Pedro Point is the closest dive site to nearby Anacapa Island, which is why some Anacapa-bound diveboats also visit San Pedro Point. Juvenile angel sharks are common in the area: look for them lying half-buried in the sandy areas. Halibut are also often seen at this site.

Lobster hunters do well in the rocky reefs, which are separated by the sandy areas. Numerous photo opportunities await photographers.

Yellow Banks Anchorage is located south of San Pedro Point and is a favorite of abalone hunters. The bottom terrain, which is made up of flat rock, extends out over a mile offshore. A fairly strong current is almost always present on the outer reef, making this an intermediate-to-advanced dive.

To the north of Yellow Banks is a large kelp bed that is well known to spearfishermen. Large sheepshead, various species of rockfish, kelp bass, and other game fish are common.

Potato Rock, west of Scorpion Anchorage, is a sea mount that comes to within ten feet of the surface. Large scallops are the rule on the wall that drops from the surface to ninety-foot waters. The wall offers photo opportunities for both the macro- and the wide-angle photographer. Exceptionally large sea stars are common in this area.

Albert's Anchorage, on the south side of the island, offers divers one of the lushest kelp beds off Santa Cruz. Perch, sea bass, rockfish, sheepshead, and yellowtail are all common around the reef. Schools of barracuda are also occasionally seen here.

Willow Anchorage, which is well-known to lobster hunters, is just about midway down the south side of the island. In addition to the "bugs," photographers also enjoy the numerous bat rays that can be found swimming through the area. It generally has the best visibility of all the sites around the island.

Gull Island is located about a third of the way down the southwest side of the island. It sits about a thousand yards offshore and truly offers something for everyone. Unlike other Channel Island pinnacles, the depth and conditions at Gull Island are moderate enough for novice divers. Lobsters are often taken around the numerous small caves in the area, as are scallops and abalones. Various types of game fish can also be found swimming under the large kelp canopy.

Purple coral can be found in some areas around Gull Island. Many people are unaware that California is home to a hard species of coral because it is not commonly seen at most sites around southern California. In addition to the purple coral, macro-photographers will find at least three different species of anemones, numerous nudibranchs, tubeworms, scallops, and an abundance of other subjects.

Potato Patch (not to be confused with Potato Rock), on the western tip of the island, is made up of a rocky reef with depths ranging between twenty and forty feet. Abalone and lobster hunters claim this to be one of the best hunting grounds around the island. Strong currents and poor visibility are usually the rule, however, making this an advanced dive.

Arch Rock is located a third of the way down the northwest side of the island and is another site frequented by hunters. Scallops are large and abundant in the rocky area close to shore.

Diablo Point, just east of Arch Rock, is a good place to see, photograph, and catch halibut. Lobsters are also known to inhabit the rocky areas.

Painted Cave, about midway between Arch Rock and the west end of the island, is worth a visit even if you don't dive it. The mouth of the cave rises over 150 feet above the water line and is a spectacular sight. Experienced charter captains will often anchor inside the cave when conditions permit. The walls of the cave appear painted due to the colored oxide on them. Water depth in the cave is about twenty feet. The bottom is sandy and barren.

Kinton Point is one of the better-known abalone sites around Santa Cruz. The uncommon Sorenson abalone is occasionally found in this area.

Black Point, north of Kinton Point, is said to have produced the biggest halibut ever found off Santa Cruz. The bottom is sandy and starts in sixty feet of water. In addition to halibut, abalones are occasionally taken in the rocky areas close to shore. Photographers should keep an eye out for bat rays, electric torpedo rays, and halibut.

50 | Dominica

It seems fitting to end this book with a destination that is just now being discovered. Dominica, not to be confused with the Dominican Republic (which is over 1,000 miles away), is located just above Martinique in the south Caribbean and offers you the chance to discover a pristine underwater environment along with some of the most beautiful above-water tropical terrain to be found anywhere in the world!

Hikers, attracted by the island's beautiful waterfalls and mountains, are rapidly discovering what Dominica has to offer. *Boiling Lake* in particular is well worth the three-hour hike, since it is one of two lakes in the world that actually boil!

Another area of the island that is most likely destined to become world famous is the *Valley of Desolation*. Known for the steam that seems to rise from the ground, the Valley of Desolation offers unique photo opportunities.

Dominica has some of the most spectacular waterfalls in the world. *Emerald Pool* is a short hike from the hotel, and offers travelers the opportunity to enjoy beautiful, isolated tropical tranquility while being serenaded by a gently cascading waterfall.

For serious explorers, *Mt. Diablotin* is the tallest peak on the island. It takes most people an average of two days to hike up the mountain.

For divers, however, it is the island's underwater charm that makes the trip worthwhile. *Hot Springs*, named after the bubbles that rise from the sandy bottom, is a unique dive. It's also shallow enough to appeal to novice divers.

The *Pinnacle* comes to within fifteen feet of the surface and is known to be excellent for macro-photographers. Numerous sponges decorate the steep drop-off. As with many dive sites that border deep water, the chances of seeing large animals while diving the Pinnacle are good.

Dominica is also becoming well-known for the spectacular wall dives that some divers claim to be "legendary." *La Bim* in particular is rapidly becoming one of the most talked about sites in the Caribbean.

The windbreaker, made by Warm Wind, is a useful accessory on any dive trip.

Go | Getting There

For more information about various dive locations, contact the resources given below or your travel agent.

1   Osborn Bank

Jon Hardy, Argo Diving Services, P.O. Box 2101, Avalon, CA 90704, (213) 510-2208.

2   The President Coolidge

M/V Coriolis, P.O. Box 84, Port Villa, Vanuatu, (678) 2899 (Fax).
Or call See & Sea Travel in San Francisco at: (415) 434-3400.

3   The R.M.S. Rhone

Trimarine Boat Company, P.O. Box 4065, St. Thomas, VI 00803, (809) 494-2490, (809) 494-5774 (Fax).

4   The Chikuzen

See the following note.

5   The Cuan Law

Traveling to the British Virgin Islands involves first getting yourself to San Juan, Puerto Rico — and then flying to Beef Island, Tortola in the British Virgin Islands. There is a hotel in the airport at San Juan. I recommend you try to arrive in San Juan at night, sleep a few hours, and then fly to Beef Island, Tortola in the morning. You will most likely travel straight from the airport to the boat, and it's much more pleasant to feel rested on your first day rather than burned out.

Trimarine Boat Company, P.O. Box 4065, St. Thomas, VI 00803, (809) 494-2490, (809) 494-5774 (Fax).

The *Cuan Law* is based in Road Town, Tortola. Cruises, however, can depart from, and travel to, any of the islands in the Caribbean.

6   Diving for Abalone

If you would like to try hunting abalone in the California area, call the diveboat *Charisma* at (310) 326-7460. They run weekly trips.

8   Angel Sharks

Argo Diving, P.O. Box 1201, Avalon, CA 90704, (310) 510-2208.

9   Conception Island

See the following note.

10   Rum Cay Island

For information about *Coral Star*, write or call:
17 Fort Royal Isle, Fort Lauderdale, FL 33308, (305) 563-1711, (800) 433-7262, (305) 563-1811 (Fax).

11   Shark Diving

The King Neptune, Catalina Diving Resorts, Dept 1DBC, P.O Box 1017, Avalon, CA 90704, (213) 510-2616.

12   Pinnipeds

Argo Diving, P.O. Box 1201, Avalon, CA 90704, (213) 510-2208.

13   Cozumel

La Ceiba Hotel, P.O. Box 284, Cozumel Q.ROO, MEXICO 77600, 52-987-2-03-79; 52-987-2-00-65 (Fax).

14   The Coronado Islands

The diveboats *Sand Dollar* and *Bottom Scratcher* both run regularly scheduled trips to the Coronado Islands.
Diving Charters, Inc., P.O. Box 6374, San Diego, CA 92106, (619) 224-4997.

15   Moray Eels

Lorraine Sadler, P.O. Box 1201, Avalon, CA 90704.

18   Palau

The Palau Pacific is located on the beach and offers vacationers luxurious accommodations and a variety of shops and restaurants. The Palau Pacific, P.O. Box 308, Koror, Palau, W.C.I. 96940.
For information about diving tours, write:
Neco Marine, P.O. Box 129, Koror, Palau, W.C.I. 96940.

19   Bonaire

Captain Don's Habitat at (800) 327-6709.
Sand Dollar Resort, 52 Georgetown Road, Bordentown, NJ 08505, (800) 345-0805.
To dial the island directly, call 011-599-7-8290.

20   Aruba

Aruba Scuba Center at 21596 or (800) 845-3483.
Red Sail Sports can be reached at 31603 or (800) 255-6425.
To call the island directly, dial 011-278-8 plus the number.

21   Curacao

Coral Cliff Hotel at 642822 or (800) 223-9815.
Curacao Seascape/Curacao Caribbean Hotel and Casino at 625000 or (800) 223-9815.
Divers Way of Curacao/Holiday Beach Hotel and Casino at 627144.
To call the island directly dial 011-599-9 and then the number.

23   Dolphin Dives

For information on diving with dolphins in the Caribbean, call or write:
Stuart Cove, Nassau Undersea Adventures, P.O. Box CB 11697, Nassau, Bahamas. U.S. Booking Number (800) 468-9876.
For information about diving with Pacific dolphins, call Argo Diving at (310) 510-2208.

24   Grand Turk

Blue WaterDivers at (809) 946-2432.
If you prefer a live-aboard diveboat, call the *Aquanaut* at (809) 946-2541.

25   Providenciales

Club Med at (800) 258-2633.
Ocean Club Condominiums at (809)-94-65880.
Treasure Beach Villas at (809)-94-64203.

26   The Caicos Islands

Dolphin Cay Divers at (809) 946-7119.

27   Silver Banks

Coral Bay Cruises, 17 Fort Royal Isle, Fort Lauderdale, FL 33308, (305) 563-1711, (305) 563-1811 (Fax).

28   The Cayman Islands

Don Foster's Dive, (800) 83-DIVER, (214) 351-3469 (Fax).
Brac Reef Beach Resort, (800) 327-3835.
Eden Rock Diving Center, (809) 949-7243.

29   Stingray City

Fisheye Photographic Services, P.O. Box 637, Grand Cayman, British West Indies, local phone: 9-3873.

30   Santa Rosa Island

Truth Aquatics runs trips to Santa Rosa out of Santa Barbara on the *Vision, Conception,* and *Truth.* Call (805) 962-1127 for information.
The *Peace,* at (805) 658-8286, and the *Scuba Luv'er,* at (805) 496-1014, run trips from the Oxnard/Ventura area.

31   Cave Diving

For information about diving the Nohoch Nachich cave system, contact Mike Madden at the Cedam Dive Center by calling 011-52-98-741339 (this line has both an answering machine and a fax on it). Or you can write Mike at his address (which is actually thirty miles away from the Dive Center):
AP117 Playa Del Carmen, Q-Roo, Mexico, 77710.
Incidentally, it is a two-and-one-half-mile hike to the caves ... the good news is, donkeys are used to carry the dive gear.

32   Ice Diving

For information about where you can obtain instruction in ice diving techniques, contact Maui Divers at (800) 227-6663, or (714) 621-5801.

33   Matagi Island, Fiji

Carol Kurop, Matagi Island, P.O. Box 83, Waiyevo, Taveuni, Fiji Islands, Telex FJ8287 Matagi, (679) 880260 (Island Telephone), (679) 880274 (Fax).

34   San Nicholas Island & Begg Rock

Diveboats *Encore* or *Charisma* at (213) 326-7460.

The *Bold Contender* also runs regularly scheduled trips to the island; they can be reached at (818) 366-2661.

Out of Santa Barbara, the *Conception, Truth,* and *Vision* all run trips to San Nicholas and can be reached at (805) 962-1127.

35   Truk Lagoon

Most divers stay at the Truk Continental. Contact: See & Sea Travel, 50 Francisco Street, Suite 205, San Francisco, CA 94133, (415) 434-3400.

36   Kwajalein

See Truk Lagoon.

37   U.S. Virgin Islands

St. John Water Sports, Box 70, Cruz Bay, St. John, USVI 00830, (809) 776-6256.

Fredericksted Above and Below, 12 Strand Street, Fredericksted, St. Croix, USVI 00840, (809) 772-3701.

St. Thomas Diving Club, Box 4976, St. Thomas, USVI 00801, (809) 774-1376.

39   Shark Frenzy

Neco Marine, P.O. Box 129, Koror, Palau, W.C.I. 96940.

40   Malibu Beach

Malibu Divers, 21231 Pacific Coast Highway, Malibu, CA 90265, (213) 456-2396.

Scubahaus, 2501 Wilshire Blvd., Los Angeles, CA 90403, (213) 828-2916.

41   The Galapagos Islands

Trimarine, P.O. Box 4065, St. Thomas, VI 00803, (809) 494-2490.

42   Jamaica

Hedonism II, P.O. Box 25, Negril, Jamaica, (809) 957-4201.
Sun Divers, (809) 973-2346.

45   The Coral Sea

Sea Safaris, (800) 821-6670, (800) 262-6670 (within California).

46   Heron Island

See & Sea Travel, 50 Francisco Street, Suite 205, San Francisco, CA 94133, (415) 434-3400.

48   Hawaii

Kona Coast Divers, 75-5614 Palani Road, Kailua-Kona, HA 96740, (800) KOA-DIVE.

49   Santa Cruz Island

Three diveboats run regularly scheduled trips to Santa Cruz Island:
eo III Dive Charters, (800) 453-5363.
The *Spectre*, (805) 483-6612 or 643-1233.
The *Peace*, (805) 658-8286.

50   Dominica

Dominica Dive Resorts, P.O. Box 34, Roseau, Dominica, (800) 328-5287, (809) 448-5680 (Fax).

Calm conditions and clear water are typical of what divers will find at Santa Cruz Island.

Index